The Power of Choice

By Carla Ives

The Power of Choice

ISBN-13: 978-1497581753

ISBN-10: 1497581753

Published by

The Eden Principle
P.O. Box 911
Mount Pleasant, MI 48804
http://theedenprinciple.wix.com/the-eden-principle
theedenprinciple@yahoo.com
989.944.2025

Edited by Jennifer Jeremiah

Printed in the United States of America

Dedication

To Doug & Sherrie Carey who began this healing journey with me one night so long ago and changed my life forever; to my amazing husband, Ron Ives, our precious children and my faithful parents who loved and supported me every step of the way. This celebration belongs to all of us.

Foreword

I met Carla Ives at a Rotary Club meeting, where she announced she was going to Uganda to help the street kids that live there. She asked if anyone was interested in going to let her know. My daughter Grace had been talking about going there sometime as well, so I figured this would be a great mother-daughter experience. Things worked out extremely well and I am proud to say we are now very good friends. Carla is a one of a kind person. She has walked humbly through all of her life's choices and trials, and with God's grace and mercy she has become the ultimate woman she is today.

This book is about Faith, Choices and Life. As a therapist it is my job to help someone understand why they made specific choices in their life. CHOICE, BELIEF, TRUTH, SHAME, ANGER, FEAR, FORGIVENESS, and SPIRIT are the many ideals addressed in this book, and they are also shared within my counseling sessions. One of the most important things in life is to believe you are valuable and lovable. Along with belief is learning to trust ourselves to make good choices. We are faced with choices every day. Some are easy some are difficult. We make good choices and we make bad choices. The Choices we make can either allow others to control our life or help us to take control of our own life. Choices in the present, past and even in our future have a bearing in our life - how they affect us, guide us, and lead us to our destiny.

God is an instrument in our lives whether we choose to believe it or not. He is active in every aspect of our life. The question is do we walk Him, do we talk with Him and most importantly do we share our thoughts or feelings with Him? He is there for our joys, sorrows, and any pain evolving from choices we made. In order to heal appropriately, the steps in Carla's book can be taken purely to heart.   This book is about all of the above, and more!

Robin K. Duthie, M.A., LPC

Table of Contents

INTRODUCTION

There is life in God's Word! It has the power to change the way we think, taking us to a new understanding of God, our relationships, our responsibilities, and ourselves. As we search the Scriptures, savoring the written Word, our hearts are softened and our values reformed. As we meditate on the truths of the Bible, they slowly become our own. We begin to possess the promise, hope, life, and faith of our Heavenly Father through the Words breathed to us on paper…

II Timothy 3:6 reminds us that, "ALL Scripture is given by inspiration of God." It is given by His breath, so that every Word we read is God-breathed. God spoke His Word into the ears of mere men who diligently recorded His truth. In reality, every Word we hear or read of God's Word tumbled from His Own lips! They are as real and powerful as if He stood before us in human form, speaking them directly into our hearts and minds.

Can you imagine? Can you imagine the impact of encountering God in a personal way; of Him speaking specifically into your very life? How would you be changed? You know in your heart even now; you could never be the same. It would be for you as it was for the first man formed by God's hand in Genesis 2:7. The man appeared to look alive, but had no life in him. Then God breathed into his body made of clay, and man became a *living* being! In the same way, the Word of God breathes life into each one of us, going into the heart and essence of who we are. And just as the man appeared lifeless until His soul was ignited by the Divine breath, so our outward lives are transformed as His Word ignites our soul. What a privilege to receive these precious and powerful Words of Life!

Jesus Christ was and IS the Word made flesh. He and His Word are inseparable. They are one. Whenever we read of our Savior in the Gospels and witness the power of His spoken Word as the crippled walked, the blind saw, the deaf heard, and the dead were raised, we should be filled with expectation. He has not changed. His Word continues to bear the full expression of His heart and power in the earth. God's Word has the power to heal, restore, deliver, and save TODAY.

I *know* this is true…

My Testimony

It was 1986, and I was desperate. After years of struggling with bouts of depression and severe panic attacks, I didn't feel I could face another day. I was weary of trying to fix my problems. I tried everything I knew to do. No amount of fasting, prayer, positive confession, repentance, or determination seemed to help. I was bound by a crippling fear that was slowly destroying me. My anxiety and unpredictable panic attacks had strained my dearest relationships with my husband and babies. It was the children that worried me most. I was often awake late into the night, worrying about the effect of my bondage on my children. What memories would they have of me? What damage was I causing them? I knew they deserved so much better than me. The times I found myself curled up in a fetal position in a corner of a room, rocking to and fro; discovering the goodbye note I had written to my family in my frenzied state, and not remembering how I ended up there frightened me the most. It HAD to stop.

I decided to run away. Locking myself in the playroom while my husband worked and my children slept, I cried out to God, "Either heal me TONIGHT or I'm going to leave. I will NOT put my babies through anymore suffering. I can't take it anymore. I QUIT!" Silence filled the playroom. Other than my weeping, you couldn't hear a sound. Then God's Voice came and filled my soul with one simple Word..."Finally!" In a moment, I suddenly understood why freedom had eluded me for so long: I was in the way! God couldn't help me because I was constantly trying to help myself. I used His Word as if I were taking a prescribed medicine rather than allowing it to be His Voice to my needy soul. Hope came. I could actually feel God's joy that I was quitting self-effort and was now ready to receive His intervention. How could I have missed this truth for so long?

As I prayed on the floor with my children's toys all around, God led me to James 5:16:

> *"Confess your trespasses [intentional or unintentional] to one another and pray for one another, that you may be **healed.**"*

God revealed this life-changing truth that it was through confession of my unintentional bondage to those who knew how to pray in faith that I would finally be healed – made completely whole in body, soul, mind, and spirit. This is what I longed for! As I snuggled into His Presence, He directed me to a new couple who had recently been attending our church. I hardly knew them, but I was determined to obey God. I called them on the telephone and learned that they had previously been part of a deliverance ministry and *loved* to pray for people. God is so good! Though very nervous and feeling ashamed, I drove to their home and parked in the driveway. Suddenly, I was overwhelmed with the familiar fear and panic. I gripped the steering wheel and debated driving away. The two faces of the dear couple appeared at the window of my car, and they lovingly encouraged me to enter their home. Once inside, they listened as I confessed my bondage openly and honestly. Then they prayed...they prayed and ministered to me with incredible love and patience until 3:00 in the morning. I had never experienced such gentleness. My beautiful Savior revealed the root of my fears and brought true freedom to my mind and heart. I left the meeting feeling more "born again" than at my conversion! The whole world looked fresh and alive. I sang at the top of my lungs and thanked God all the way home. I was HEALED!

A day later, I knew that there was still more work to be done. I WAS healed, but the healing had to be worked into every pattern, thought, and aspect of my life. Years of bondage had resulted in negative thought and behavior patterns that I easily returned to in times of trouble. This is when I learned the power of God's Word. I threw myself into the study of God's Word. I meditated on it day and night. I used every moment that my children slept to absorb more Scripture. I couldn't seem to get enough! I had an insatiable hunger. And as I read, meditated, and studied the Bible, my mind was being renewed. With no fleshly effort, my thoughts were transformed. I began to think differently about myself, God, and everyone else. I responded differently to the stress of life. Over time, I became softer, less controlling, and experienced new depths of love. It was a delightful journey that I am continuing to this day.

Remember...

I am a pastor, not a licensed counselor. I don't pretend to have all of the training these dedicated men and women have. I'm not saying you won't need their help in some way on your healing journey. You may, or you may not; let God lead you. What I am sharing with you on the pages of this book is my own experience, understanding, and revelation received at the feet of Jesus while recovering from my brokenness. Hidden in these pages are a few isolated experiences in my otherwise wonderful life that changed who I was, momentarily took away my ability to choose, and set me on a path of healing. I feel your pain; I've walked your road, and I am cheering you on as you take hold of the freedom Christ purchased for you.

Living Free,

Carla Ives

CHAPTER ONE

Restoration of Choice

There are many people like me. They are survivors. In painful moments of life, they developed survival skills to protect themselves. These skills held them together and brought them through the difficulties, but today these same "skills" have become a bondage to them. They are chained to negative thoughts and behaviors that control their decisions and every aspect of life. The skills—ones they developed to survive abuse, critical words, rejection, neglect, war, or abandonment—are now slowly destroying them. The chains are strong, and they cannot live without them. Yet, they dream of freedom...

When people develop negative thought patterns in their minds, they make poor decisions that ultimately separate them from the blessings of God. They are "chained" to their past experiences and abusers and feel unable to control their lives or circumstances. They hate the feeling of powerlessness most of all. Powerlessness is equated to pain...to being controlled...to being silenced. They hate weakness and fight it wherever they find it, especially in themselves. They would rather deny the emotion than feel it. Without realizing it, they are no longer able to make healthy decisions. The past chooses for them, just as those who hurt them and the experiences of life chose for them before. The past tells them to stay in unhealthy relationships—to give up or run away or to give themselves to destructive/addictive lifestyles. The hurt inside tells them to reject all blessings, suspect all kindness, and sabotage any good thing that comes their way. Thus they are hindered in relationships, in progress at school or work, and in their own emotional and/or spiritual growth. They do not know that Christ came to break EVERY chain—past, present, and future!

Pain Isn't A New Experience.

If any people on earth can understand pain, abuse, and rejection, it is the people of Israel! Throughout history, they have known long seasons of slavery, betrayal, war, death, and destruction. They were in the worst oppression they had ever known when Moses came by God's direction to deliver them. But though they were legally, physically, and completely set free from slavery and the hostile abusers who controlled them, their minds and emotions were not. They stumbled through their wilderness journey like lambs to the slaughter. They doubted God's Word, disobeyed His commands, and challenged His leaders. As Moses faced the wounded mass at the end of his earthly ministry, he challenged them to make a choice:

"I call heaven and earth as witnesses today against you, that I have set before you, life and death, blessing and cursing; therefore **choose life,** that both you and your descendants may live; that you may love the Lord your God, that you may obey His voice, and that you may cling to Him, for He is your life and the length of your days; and that you may dwell in the land which the Lord swore to your fathers, to Abraham, Isaac, and Jacob, to give them." (Deuteronomy 30:19-20)

Offering Israel this choice of life or death was a powerful gift. Their taskmasters of the past had made every decision for them. Their pain forced them to yield to the demands of their enemies. When they had perhaps thought of rising up against their oppressors, they were punished in ungodly ways that broke their spirit of resistance and destroyed their ability to choose. Life chose for them. They were afraid to think for themselves. They were afraid to make mistakes again. They had done everything they could to position themselves so that their Christian leader would make all of the decisions for them for over 40 years. They were free—but not *too* free. Then Moses put the weight of all future decisions for their lives and relationship with God on them.

Moses had given the people God's Word. He had taught them the statutes and commands of His law. He had served as mediator between man and God and presided as Judge over their disputes. It was time for them to stand on their own. When Moses challenged them to choose, he was teaching them five subtle truths:

1) You are NO LONGER under the dominion of the enemy. You are free!

2) You know God's Word and power for yourselves.

3) You don't need a mediator anymore; you can go to God yourselves.

4) You have the right and privilege to CHOOSE.

5) You have the ability to make the right choice.

God is giving you the same "gift" today. **He is restoring your right to CHOOSE**. The past, the abuser, and the experiences of life no longer have to choose your course. Your emotion no longer has to rule your mind or behavior. If you have received Jesus as Lord and Savior, you are NO LONGER a slave to sin. You know God's Word—He breathes inside of you! You no longer need a mediator; you can go to God for yourself. You have the right, privilege, and ability to CHOOSE. Now **you** must choose what you will do with this incredible privilege.

This is the first hurdle we must pass before we can move forward with our lives. This is where many determine to stay "stuck" in the cycles, behaviors, and hopelessness of the past. They don't want to choose. It's too frightening, requires too much energy, and is simply too much work. They want others to choose for them. If someone else chooses for me and is wrong, I have them to blame. The victim mentality tells us, "If I remain helpless, no one will expect much from me; and therefore, I don't have to risk trying something and failing." To make a choice, I will have to stop hiding behind a victim mentality. Victims live at the mercy of their captors, who make all choices for them. A victim is exempt from responsibility and focuses only on survival. Making a choice forces me to declare that I am a victim no longer—I am going to take life by the horns and live it! This opens me to risk of failure, loss, or injury. In the end, many of us decide to stay hidden in our pasts.

It is when we choose to believe God's Word concerning every area of our lives that we are changed. For some, this will require relearning how to take responsibility for the decisions made every day. We must own and understand the impact of the perspectives, attitudes, speech, or behaviors we choose to vent. No more denying, avoiding, or ignoring our responsibility for the choices we make each day. Our decisions determine our future and touch the lives of those closest to us. True freedom and maturity is demonstrated by a willingness to own our decisions.

The Choice is YOURS...

Israel struggled with Moses's challenge over the years. The fruit of their decisions followed them into the Promised Land and brought them both joy and pain. When they consciously chose to worship and obey God, they experienced years of abundance, protection, victory, and peace. When they refused to take responsibility for their choices but rather followed leaders blindly (allowing them to be led away from God), they experienced years of sin, struggle, lack, and suffering. Their personal choices impacted future generations.

"Now therefore, fear the Lord, serve Him in sincerity and in truth, and put away the false gods which your fathers served on the other side of the River and in Egypt. Serve the Lord! And if it seems evil to you to serve the Lord, **choose for yourselves** this day whom you will serve, whether the gods which your fathers served that were on the other side of the River, or the gods of the Amorites, in whose land you dwell. But as for me and my house, we will serve the Lord." (Joshua 24:14-25)

Before ending his season on earth, Joshua again challenged the Israelites to CHOOSE. His challenge was very clear and direct. It was as if he were saying in our modern language, "Israel, you can either continue to allow the gods of your past—the pain, abuse, fear, anger, bitterness, or sorrow of your past—to rule your thoughts, emotions, and behaviors OR you can DECIDE to obey God. Whatever you decide will determine your future. The choice is completely yours!

Clearly Defining the Choices We Must Make...

The word "god" or "idol" used in this Scripture is something that rules and governs our lives. Whatever motivates our decisions—whatever determines the choices we make—is truly our "god." These gods are not always made of expensive gold or carved wood; they are made of the fabric of our brokenness. Our painful memories, damaged emotions, and destructive behaviors or addictions now rule our lives. We may look for others to choose for us, giving power to mere men or women to make decisions concerning how we dress and speak, where we go and what we do. This is idolatry. Without realizing it, we have bowed to other "gods" that can only add to our suffering.

When we receive Jesus as Lord and Savior of our lives, we place Him as the ONLY God we will bow to. He becomes the Supreme Authority of our daily existence. Yet even then, He does not choose FOR us. He tells us His thoughts and reveals His will and Word, but He allows US to choose what we will do with the information. This is not forced servitude that robs us of all dignity and choice. Instead, God restores our right to choose.

This is good news to people like me! I was once bound by the "gods" of the first man who sexually abused me. He was a teenage boy who lived near our family when I was growing up. He had always been polite to me or even ignored me in the past. One day when my father was being rushed to the hospital in an ambulance, my mother sent my sister and me to his family's home to be taken care of. In a panic, holding my sister's hand, I ran to their house and banged on the door. They weren't home...but their teenage son was. I don't remember all of the details to this day; I was only nine years old. I do, however, remember him inviting us into his bedroom where he showed us pornographic magazines while touching us—me in particular. He wasn't an evil young man; he was simply bound by sin. I was ashamed. I don't remember saying anything. I shut down, as many children in these circumstances do. I hid the episode in my heart and did not speak of it again until I became a Christian years later.

Though I hated what the boy did to me and felt terribly ashamed, I could not seem to block out the images he had put before me. The "gods" of my abuser had become my own. A gate had been opened to pornography in my little heart and mind, and I began a long struggle with the issue. It was a silent battle that I revealed to no one. Regardless of the shame that haunted me, I seemed drawn to look at magazines, read books, and watch television shows or movies that fed the addiction. The world was happy to oblige me with the "soap operas," romance novels, and magazine racks. I eventually gave my life to Christ and received healing from the abuse; but the images in my mind lived on. I was too ashamed to tell anyone. My understanding was that this was a problem for men. To be a young woman struggling with the issue seemed exceptionally wrong. I told no one. I hid the issue from my husband for fear he would be hurt or repulsed by it. It was my one secret sin...and eventually my one secret deliverance. Jesus mercifully met me where I was and set me free from pornography without the support of other believers. It took time for my mind to be totally freed of the images, but my deliverance was real and lasting.

Personal Choice Determines Personal Outcome!

God has given you an incredible ability to make decisions. You were made in His image. You have the mind of Christ. No matter your history, experience, stature, or IQ, you have the legal authority and ability to choose. No one can ever take this privilege from you. You can choose to change the direction of your life this very moment!

Identifying the source of decisions made in the past, you may have to ask yourself several questions. These questions should be asked patiently; don't try to hurry yourself in this healing process. I know how this works; I've been there. With the help of the Holy Spirit, simply open your mind and heart to these questions. The questions might be:

- Have you experienced the "gods" of the abusers of your past?

- Do you find yourself becoming tempted or ensnared by the same bondage issues of the abusers who once brought you so much pain?

If you responded "yes" to the above questions, you may be struggling with the same alcoholism that your parent struggled with. You may be involved in the same sexual addictions as the one who once abused you. You may have a temper that hurts those you love just as someone's temper once wounded you. This is what it is to be under the dominion of an abuser's "god." But YOU have another GOD—THE Only God!

It is Time!

It is time to tear down the idols and burn every false "god" in the fire of God's Presence! This deliverance begins the moment you understand your ability to choose. When you accept a revelation of the freedom you have received in Christ Jesus, you will be able to take hold of your ability to choose, and choose your way to life!

"By faith, Moses, when he became of age, refused to be called the son of Pharaoh's daughter, **choosing rather** to suffer affliction with the people of God than to enjoy the passing pleasures of sin, esteeming the reproach of Christ greater riches than the treasures in Egypt; for he looked to the reward." (Hebrews 11:24-25)

The challenge of personal choice began in Moses's life long before he presented it to the Israelites. The Book of

Hebrews tells us that Moses *chose* (took for himself; preferred) to suffer affliction with God's people rather than enjoy the pleasures of sin for a season. His return to Egypt required a conscious decision to obey the command of God rather than the fear of death. These verses share his ultimate decision to value obedience to God above all the treasures of Egypt. Any suffering experienced in the process or course of this decision was deemed acceptable as long as he was able to CHOOSE.

Today, YOU are Confronted with the Same Choice.

Your own decision to "step past the past" and begin to move forward with your life is a demonstration of your faith in Christ. Forward motion often meets with resistance, but you will be able to persevere when you know YOU chose the course. You are on a quest to complete, manifested freedom and are willing to endure suffering in order to take hold of it.

The truth is that many of you will never find the strength to move forward on your own. The past seems too big to "step over." In these situations, Psalm 25 becomes even more precious. Here you are assured that God willingly instructs you, helping you to make the right decision every time. All you have to do is revere/respect Him. Before making a decision, you whisper a prayer. You wait on God. He never ignores your cry!

"Who is the man [woman] that fears [respects] the Lord? Him [her] shall He teach in the way He chooses. He [she] himself [herself] shall dwell in prosperity, and his [her] descendants shall inherit the earth. The secret of the Lord is with those who fear [revere] Him, and he will show them His covenant. My eyes are ever toward the Lord, for He shall pluck my feet out of the net." (Psalm 25:12-15)

Choosing to seek God for His counsel is the next step in the freedom process. We must let Him help us. This means admitting that we cannot make all of life's decisions on our own. We are not as strong or independent as others think we are. We are vulnerable. We don't know the right thing to do in every situation. We are willing to receive the counsel and help of One Who knows far more than us. It is not easy to place yourself in such a place of vulnerability, but it is a necessity for moving forward. There comes a moment in each person's life when they face a river too wide, too fast, and too unknown to navigate themselves. Like it or not, we all **need** God!

"Trust in the Lord with all your heart, and lean not on your own understanding; In all your ways acknowledge Him and He shall direct your paths. Do not be wise in your own eyes; Fear [revere] the Lord and depart from evil It will be health to your flesh, and strength to your bones." (Proverbs 3:5-8)

You Have More Options Than You Realize!

I can still remember the incredible feeling of freedom that I had the day I finally understood that I was no longer at the mercy of my past, my abusers, or my own stupid decisions. Even if I chose my way into a bad situation, I could now choose my way out of it and into something good! And just because someone did something bad to me, I didn't have to repeat the painful cycle, harming myself or others. I could choose to receive the help needed to be healed and walk in wholeness.

"Do not envy the oppressor, and **choose none of his ways**…" (Proverbs 3:31).

In giving this command, God implies the wonderful option that we need never to envy or choose the ways of those who abused or misused us. The term "oppressor" is defined as any individual who is violent, does wrong, or is

34

cruel and unjust. In His subtle way, God tells us that we can choose whether or not we will be ruled by the "gods" of our abusers. We don't have to repeat their mistakes! We can choose to be honest and allow others to help us. We can learn new ways of speech, behavior, and thinking as we receive God's help and counsel. His Word has the power to retrain our minds so we can think differently!

Most of us spend years remembering, evaluating, and trying to understand our pasts. Yet the painful truth is that we can never change any of it. No matter how angry or sad we are; no matter how much we wish it would never have happened; no matter how hard we try to forget—the past IS. It is our history. It happened. It can never be changed. There comes a point for every child of God when they must let the past go and move on with their lives. We cannot change yesterday, BUT we can make decisions that will shape our today and tomorrows!

There will be brief moments of "looking back" as we continue this process of change. These moments will be for the purpose of exposing and breaking any lingering chains that control our decisions and behaviors today. We are breaking free from the web of the "spider" that nearly destroyed us. We are throwing off the chains that hinder us. We are getting ready to run free!

As we take this freedom journey together, remember that God is GOD. He is not like any other person you have ever known. He is not an abuser. He is slow to anger and abounding in mercy. He is full of tenderness. He is patient. He never manipulates or controls mankind. He gives counsel and allows us to choose how we will respond to the information. What He gives, He gives COMPLETELY. The right and ability to choose is yours!

I encourage you take some time to pray now. Lay your past at the feet of Jesus. You may want to ask a counselor, friend, or pastor to do this with you. This will give you the support and accountability needed to move on. We can't do life alone, no matter how much we wish we could! After you have decided to leave your past with Jesus, you'll next have to choose NOT to go back and reclaim it. Let it go. Let God and others help you. Live in the moment. Let God show you what He has for you NOW.

CHAPTER TWO

Choosing to Believe

Who IS God? What IS He like? Almost everyone in the world has an opinion concerning the character of God—if they acknowledge His existence. To one, He is the most loving, caring Father a child could have; to another, He is the demanding, relentless dictator they hope to escape. God looks different to different people because of the "lenses" they wear. Whether they realize it or not, their view of God is often shaped and confused by the experiences of life. Often they attribute the character of the significant males in their lives to Him simply because He is "HE." Because God is an authority figure, they attribute the attitudes and reactions of other authority figures in their lives to Him. The opinions of others coupled with the religious teachings and images on television complete their picture of the Creator. To say the least, their picture is confused!

When I was a little girl, we had several boxes of puzzles with hundreds of tiny pieces. Over time, the pieces got mixed up, and it became almost impossible to put the puzzles together. The picture didn't make sense when the pieces were from another box or positioned wrong. The only way to do the puzzle correctly was to take the time and effort to separate all of the pieces and put them into their own boxes. Only when we had the pieces belonging to the actual puzzle could we finally see the promised picture. It was a task filled with tedious detail and was often frustrating, but the sorting was absolutely necessary to achieve the desired end. So it is with your present journey.

To continue your healing process, you will have to patiently endure a season of revelation. You will have to unravel the lies from the truth you've believed all of these years. You will have to sort out the pieces of your past and present. You will have to carefully separate the truth from your feelings and wrong perceptions. It will be tedious, frustrating at times, and perhaps a little discouraging—but it is necessary to the process. It is only the knowledge of TRUTH that sets us free!

If you do not know God for Who He truly IS, your ability to make quality decisions is hindered. Think of the man who thinks God demands perfection. He will try to "fix" his problems himself, allowing no one to help him. Then there's the woman who sees God as the earthly father who abused her; she will live in stark fear of failing Him. A wrong view of the mercy of God may cause an ignorant soul to continue in sin, while an incorrect understanding of his wrath may cause an insecure person to run away. The way you see God affects many of the decisions you make every day.

There is only one true source for learning God's character. The Bible is His letter, whispered into the ears of men and recorded for mankind. All of scripture is "God-breathed." To read the Bible is to hear a description and definition of God from His Own mouth! It is only through the study of the Word of God that we are able to know Him as He truly is.

Knowing God in TRUTH is vital to your spiritual growth. You must allow your preconceived ideas formed by past experiences and the opinion of man concerning His heart and ways to be challenged and the lies discarded if you are going to embrace God as GOD. As you learn of His true love, kindness, and goodness revealed in the scriptures, you will know a new confidence in His Presence. This will allow you to enter into greater intimacy of relationship with your Savior, able to receive His counsel and direction for the decisions you make every day. No longer will you make decisions that bring hardship to others or yourself! Every aspect of your life personally, socially, at work, and at play will be altered by the revelations you receive in God's Word.

Seeing Through Broken Lenses...

Picture God walking with mankind in the midst of a beautiful world, unspoiled by sin. Everything is "good." There is nothing to fear. There is plentiful supply. Love is the strongest emotion, and there is no definition for "hate." The man and woman know their Heavenly Father gave them this gift of life. They are able to see Him face-to-face and talk with Him in the cool of the day (Genesis 1 & 2).

While walking through the garden one day, they are confronted by a snake slithering in a tree. He has positioned himself where he can best draw attention to the forbidden fruit of the Tree of the Knowledge of Good and Evil. The man and woman's first mistake was stopping to look. They should have passed by the tree, regardless of the snake. The One who had loved and given them so much had only asked that they ignore this tree. Yet they stopped. They looked. They listened.

As soon as the serpent captured their attention, he began to weave a web of lies to ensnare them. As a spider weaves a web to capture the fly, then traps it with more webbing until it cannot leave, so the serpent ensnared the first couple. He began with subtle insinuations..."Has God REALLY said...???" He insinuated that God was not fair—that He was actually "holding out" on them! He accused God of lying to them. He convinced them that unless they disobeyed God and ate the forbidden fruit, they could never be "like God," knowing good and evil. **The longer they listened, the more the lies sounded like truth.** They buckled under the weight of deception and ate.

What did they eat? For decades, mankind has interpreted the "forbidden fruit" as an apple. From books, to movies, to cartoons, it is almost always an apple that is eaten that day. Close your eyes even now and picture the scene...what do YOU see? Most people envision a bright red apple. Yet, nowhere in scripture are we told it was an apple that was eaten that day! Generations have made this assumption based only on the opinion and word pictures of past generations. There is no actual proof of this, and therefore, it cannot be accepted as true. Yet we believe it. We believe something that may not be true because others have told us it was true. If we do this with so small an issue, what do we do with the bigger issues of life? How many decisions do we make each day based on false information??? No wonder we make wrong decisions!

The first couple chose to listen to the lies of the serpent. They discarded the time spent with their Father. They pushed aside thoughts of His Word and kindness. They lived only for that moment of time. They based their next decision on what they felt, saw, and heard in that moment. Their decision cost them everything. They chose to believe the lies of the serpent named Satan, which brought them sin, suffering, and ultimate separation from God.

"Now the serpent was more cunning than any beast of the field which the Lord God had made. And he said to the woman, 'Has God indeed said, 'You shall not eat of every tree of the garden'?' And the woman said to the serpent, 'We may eat the fruit of the trees of the garden; but of the fruit of the tree which in is in the midst of the garden, God has said, 'You shall not eat it, nor shall you touch it, lest you die'.' Then the serpent said to the woman, 'You will not surely die. For God knows that in the day you eat of it your eyes will be opened, and you will be like God, knowing good and evil.' So when the woman saw that the tree was good for food, that it was pleasant to the eyes, and a tree desirable to make one wise, she took of its fruit and ate. She also gave to her husband with her, and he ate. Then the eyes of them both were opened, and they knew that they were naked; and they sewed fig leaves together and made themselves coverings." (Genesis 3:1-7)

Most of us feel angry when we read this Bible account. What was wrong with them? How could they so easily ignore God's one request? How could they toss aside the love and goodness shown to them? How could they believe such ridiculous lies about their wonderful Creator? **Yet we do the same thing.** We read of God's faithfulness and mercy, yet we doubt Him as soon as we hear a negative report. We receive His provision for a need, and then question His ability or willingness to help us when confronted with a new need. In truth, we waver in faith for the same reason original man did: we believe a lie about the One we love.

When we choose to "believe" the experiences of life, the opinions of man, or the teachings of those who know God only in theory, we will have difficulty making sound decisions. Experiences often contradict each other, opinions change, and religious teachings are altered over time. If our foundation for decision-making is constantly shifting and changing, how can we make solid decisions that will add to our lives? Our wrong belief systems become an insecure foundation for making judgments, leaving our emotions of the moment our final compass. No wonder we make so many decisions that bring trouble and confusion to our lives!

This then confronts us with our first decision that MUST be made before all others: What will you base your decisions on? Will it be the experiences of life, opinions of others, and past religious training OR on the TRUTH of God's Word? God's Word never changes, comes directly from the Source, and supersedes all of life's experiences. It has been tried and tested for over 2,000 years and has never failed. Truth has endured. There are millions of testimonies all over the world to verify the truth of God's Word. In a shifting, changing, and confused world, the Bible is unchanging and secure.

A Personal Example

Perhaps my testimony will help you to understand the importance of this challenge. I can remember being a young girl of perhaps nine years. My mother had taken my father to a hospital in Cleveland, Ohio for a major surgery that they hoped would save his life and end his years of pain. Things went wrong, and they were gone for many weeks. I was afraid. When my father did return, he was still recovering, and things became very different in our home. In my little girl view, the world turned upside-down, and nothing felt secure. I didn't know what to do. At the same time, I was dealing with the abuse that happened with the neighbor boy. I didn't know who to talk to about all of these things.

I finally went to my Sunday School teacher at the Baptist church my family attended. After class one Sunday morning, I told her everything that had happened and asked her to help me. She smiled and patted me on the shoulder. She said in essence, "God is watching you from far away to see if you will be a good girl. If you're a good girl, someday you'll go to heaven and everything will be better. You just keep on praying." I remember thinking, "Why should I pray if God isn't going to help me?" A doubt concerning God's goodness and love crept into my heart that caused me to walk away from God years later. I accepted the teacher's view of God as my own…a view of God as far away, unconcerned about my problems, and unable to help me. Of course, this is not a true view of God; but for many years, I accepted it as true. Sure, I cried out to Him in times of desperation, but I expected nothing from Him.

Each of us needs to determine where our view of God came from. Then, we need to seek out the truth concerning Who He really is.

Are We Making Fair Judgments?

No one likes to be judged unfairly or to be falsely accused! I once knew a young teen girl, who was consistently called embarrassing names by a significant family member. This person would sometimes insist that she walk across the room so he could determine by the way she walked if she had been "fooling around" with a guy that day. Each time, she felt completely humiliated and her face would burn. At this point in her life, she was actually a good girl. But eventually, she felt defeated by the constant insinuation that she was "bad" and stopped fighting the temptation. Why did it matter? She was already branded as a "bad girl." The unfair judgment altered her self-image and made her want to fail. She stopped trying to defend herself and simply became what the world accused her of being.

Thankfully, God is not like a man (or woman)! Our wrong perceptions and false accusations don't alter His Self-view or behavior at all. He is the same God yesterday, today, and forever. But He feels the pain of our unfair judgments just as much as you or I would. He wants to be known for Who He really is. He has written an entire Book in His defense! Doesn't He deserve the chance to introduce Himself to us? To right the wrongs believed about Him?

It's a "Trust Issue."

When Adam and Eve believed a lie about God, something happened to the harmony of their home because distrust entered their relationship. If they couldn't trust God, they couldn't trust one another. The serpent lied about God and their own value, and now they lied about themselves and one another. Neither took personal responsibility for his or her sin. The experience destroyed their mutual trust and violated their pure love for one another. Once trust was gone, a legacy of blaming, using, and hurting the people we love was established. You see it carried into the lives of their first two sons, Cain and Abel, in Genesis 4. Once trust was violated, their wonderful connection with God and one another was damaged. This resulted in broken intimacy.

"And they heard the sound of the Lord God walking in the garden in the cool of the day, and Adam and his wife hid themselves from the presence of the Lord God and the trees of the garden. Then the Lord God called Adam and said to him, 'Where are you?' So he said, 'I heard your voice in the garden, and I was afraid because I was naked; and I hid myself.' And He said, 'Who told you that you were naked? Have you eaten from the tree of which I commanded you that you should not eat?' Then the man said, 'The woman You gave to be with me, she gave me of the tree, and I ate.' And the Lord God said to the woman, 'What is this you have done?' The woman said, 'The serpent deceived me, and I ate.'" (Genesis 3:8-13)

Trust is the foundation of all relationships. When we fail to trust others, we become easy prey for the enemy. He can say anything, and we think it could be true. We begin to believe what we see and hear about the person more than we believe the person him/herself. We do the same to God. Our foundation of broken trust opens us to doubt and false belief systems about Him. Our walk with Him is based more upon experience and feeling than on the truth of His Word. We are afraid to trust Him because of something the enemy did or provoked us to do. The enemy damaged our ability to trust.

It's very easy to know if you have "trust issues." Do you restrain yourself from getting "too close" to others? Do you avoid showing or even feeling emotion? Are you quick to believe a bad report about someone you love? Are you tortured with fear of them hurting or abandoning you? Your inability to trust will impact all of your decisions, causing pain to you and those you love.

The Eve of My Wedding

The night before I married my handsome husband was miserable for me. I remember lying in bed, imagining all of the things that could go wrong the next day. I tossed and turned, excited and yet afraid of the morning. Finally, I pulled two strips of paper from my desk and wrote two lists. The first was a list of the kind of wife I wanted to be. I would greet him with a kiss. I would make sure I looked and smelled good when he came home from work each day. I would make a home for us. My pen flowed with my good intentions. I was so in love with Ron!

When the first list was finished and placed carefully in the back of my Bible, I began the second list. The title of this page was: What I Will Do When Ron Leaves Me. Though we were being married the next morning, I already expected him to grow weary of me and leave one day. I knew that once he lived with me and saw me as I really was, he would quickly fall out of love with me. I didn't trust him to stay. To protect myself, I created this back-up plan and kept it in the back of my Bible for several years. I had learned to trust no man. I needed to prepare for the worst.

Sadly, my lack of trust in Ron's love and commitment to me opened us to many spiritual attacks and arguments. It took me years before I truly believed he loved me and would stay. There were many times I packed HIS bags so he could leave after a difficult conversation. If he didn't seem excited enough to be with me, I assumed he was growing tired of me. If he didn't touch me every day, I assumed he wasn't attracted to me anymore. This led to a very rocky road in the early years of our marriage. And none of my fears were justified. Today, we've been married for over 30 years, and Ron has never left me for anything other than work. Our life together is rich and full. The years of torment I experienced were so unnecessary!

We need to deal with the trust issues of our lives for the sake of those who love us. They deserve to be known for who they truly are. If we don't want to confront our issues for our own sakes, can we do it for the ones we love?

Wrong Belief Systems & Religious Mindsets

Some of our trust issues stem from wrong biblical teaching. We were raised in a religious atmosphere of control and manipulation. Our original teachers introduced God as a fearsome dictator rather than a loving Father. We were hammered with the dos and don'ts of scripture, focusing on the laws of God more than the love of God. Man's laws were mingled in with scriptural dictates, and we became confused. The Christian life became impossible to live, and Christ seemed impossible to please. We struggled with guilt and condemnation as we failed to measure up to His expectations day after day.

It is time to find out for yourself what the Bible teaches!

"For the kingdom of heaven is like a man traveling to an afar country, who called his own servants and delivered his good to them. And to one he gave five talents, to another two, and too another one, to each according to his own ability; and immediately he went on a journey. Then he who had received the five talents went and traded with them, and made another five talents. And likewise he who had received two gained two more also. But he who had received one went and dug in the ground, and hid his lord's money.

After a long time, the lord of those servants came and settled accounts with them. So he who had received five talents came and brought five other talents, saying, 'Lord, you delivered to me five talents; look, I have gained five more talents besides them.' His lord said to him, 'Well done, good and faithful servant; you were faithful over a few things, I will make you ruler over many things. Enter into the joy of your lord.' He also who had received two talents came and said, 'Lord, you delivered to me two talents; look, I have gained two more talents besides them.' His Lord said to him, 'Well done, good and faithful servant; you have been faithful over a few things, I will make you ruler over many things. Enter into the joy of your lord.'

Then he who had received the one talent came and said, 'Lord, I knew you to be a hard man, reaping where you have not sown, and gathering where you have not scattered seed. And I was afraid and went and hid your talent in the ground. Look, there you have what is yours.' But his lord answered and said to him, 'You wicked and lazy servant, you knew that I reap where I have not sown, and gather where I have not scattered seed. So you ought to have deposited my money with the bankers, and at my coming I would have received back my own with interest. Therefore, take the talent from him, and give it to him who has ten talents. For to everyone who has, more will be given and he will have abundance; but from him who does not have, even what he has will be taken away.'" (Matthew 25:14-29)

For over twenty years, I read this story wrong. When I read these verses, I interpreted it to say that the Master temporarily entrusted some of his money (talents) to three servants. Later, he returned to see what they had done with it before reclaiming it. This is a wrong interpretation of the scripture made by my believing the opinions of others and religious training of my youth. The experiences of life seemed to justify the interpretation, and it seemed just as the third servant voiced, "God only gave to test me with what was given...then would ultimately take it away." I saw God as more of "taker" than a "giver." With these "lenses," the previous interpretation of the passage seemed true.

I was wrong. I taught the scripture wrong for years. When I actually took the time to study it for myself, I learned that the Master GAVE the servants the money. The word "gave" means he that he utterly yielded, surrendered, bestowed, and truly gave the money to them! He had no intention of taking it back. It was a gift given. He didn't return to reclaim the money, for he never requested it. The Bible does not ever record that the Master took the money back. What he gave, he gave completely. It was the servant's money now. He only returned to see what they had done with it. When he saw the faithfulness of the first two to use the given gift, he increased the gift. He GAVE even more! This interpretation of the passage sheds a whole new light on the Master. He wasn't the hard man that the third servant believed. He was a giving, trusting man, and desired only to bless his servants.

The third servant in the parable had a wrong perception of the Master that cost him greatly. He made a decision to bury his gift in the dirt and ignore it because he thought the Master would take it from him. Why get excited about something you think will be taken away? Why spend time, energy, and emotion on a dream you think will never come to pass? The servant's wrong perception of the Master caused him to make a wrong decision with his gift. His wrong decision brought negative consequences to his life. It impacted his entire future!

Your wrong perception of God will cause you to make wrong decisions, bringing negative consequences into your life. It is important to re-evaluate your belief system concerning the Father, Son, and Holy Spirit. Without realizing it, you are making decisions every day based on what you believe about God. What is YOUR perception of God? Do you see Him as a Giver or Taker; a Father or Dictator; a Savior or Judge; as Love or Condemnation?

My determination to know God and His Word in simplicity and truth has led to many lengthy Bible studies over the years. I have read the Bible from cover-to-cover more times than I can count. I once did a two-year study on the character of God, journaling scriptural descriptions of His face, voice, heart, and perspectives. Another time, I studied the word "all" for over a year. I learned that He is ALL powerful, ALL knowing, and ALL sufficient for me! Each study opened my mind and heart to God in a greater way. The truth set me free to trust again! As my relationship with God grew, all of the other relationships in my life benefited as well.

We Need Help to Trust Again!

"However, when He, the Spirit of truth, has come, He will guide you into all truth; for He will not speak on His own authority, but whatever He hears He will speak and He will tell you things to come. He will glorify Me, for He will take of what is Mine and declare it to you. All things that the Father has are Mine. Therefore, I said that He will take of Mine and declare it to you." (John 16:13-15)

Jesus promised that He would send His Spirit to reveal Himself to mankind. He never intended to be a mystery to His Friends. He wanted them to KNOW Him. The

Holy Spirit is here on earth to reveal TRUTH to us. We can ask Him to reveal the mind, character, heart, and ways of God to us. We can invite Him, the Spirit of Grace, to influence our hearts to believe only the TRUTH about God. As we read the scriptures, we can ask Him to teach us. How much better to allow God to interpret His Words for Himself!

This is a decision only you can make. Only you can choose to ask for help. Only you can choose to receive the help you need. Stop right now and invite the Holy Spirit to teach you. Invite Him to reveal truth to you concerning God and His ways. Lay a wrong belief system at His feet. Let Him sweep away the wrong perceptions. Let Him cleanse you from wrong judgments made about God or man. Study the scriptures to learn what God Himself said about the issue. Read it as it is written, with the help of the Holy Spirit. Strip the scripture of all previous interpretations made out of past experiences, religious training, or the opinions of man. What does it REALLY say?

"Beloved, let us love one another, for love is of God; and everyone who loves is born of God and KNOWS God. He who does not love does not KNOW God, for God is love. In this is the love of God was manifested toward us, that God has sent His only begotten Son into the world, that we might live through Him. In this is love, not that we loved God, but that He loved us and sent His Son to be the propitiation for our sins.

Beloved, if God so loved us, we also ought to love one another. No one has seen God at any time. If we love one another, God abides in us, and His love has been perfected in us. But this we KNOW that we abide in Him, and He in us, because He has given us of His Spirit. And we have seen and testify that the Father has sent the Son as Savior of the world. Whoever confesses that Jesus is the Son of God, God abides in him, and he in God. And we have KNOWN and believed the love that God has for us. God is love, and he who abides in love abides in God, and God in him. Love has been perfected among us in this: that we may have boldness in the day of judgment; because as He is, so are we in this world.

There is no fear in love; but perfect love casts out fear, because fear involves torment. But he who fears has not been made perfect in love. 'We love Him' because He first loved us. If someone says, 'I love God,' and hates his brother, he is a liar; for he who does not love his brother whom he has seen, how can he love God whom he has not seen? And this commandment we have from Him; that he who loves God must love his brother also." (I John 4:11-21)

Are You Willing to Hear the Truth?

It doesn't take discernment to understand what this passage of scripture teaches. God IS Love. If we do not know Him as Love, we do not KNOW Him. If we don't know Him as Love, we cannot give Love to others. We cannot give what we do not have! It is as if our Father ripped open His heart and poured it upon John the Apostle. He wanted us to know that we are loved by Him...that He proved His love by sacrificing His Son, Jesus. He reminded us that He sacrificed to redeem us from sin and restore us to fellowship with Him at a time when we didn't even want Him! We denied Him. We distrusted Him. Yet He never changed in His heart towards us. Love was, and has always been, the compelling force of His interaction with man—His intervention for man.

We cannot trust if we do not know the truth. We cannot love if we do not trust. We are missing the beauty of the Christian life and our Divine purpose if we fail to love! Nothing else will satisfy. Our quest for truth is where the healing process truly begins. God gave specific guidelines in this scripture for Love so that we would be able to clearly evaluate whether or not we were experiencing it. Perfect love casts out fear. If we are fearful of God's unwillingness or inability to help or love us—if we are tormented by fear and anxieties in our mind and emotions—we do not KNOW

God. This revelation drives us to a search for truth. Who IS God? How DOES He feel about us? Do we actually KNOW God, or have we simply heard a lot about Him?

This scripture passage also asserts that failure to KNOW God decreases our ability to love others. If we cannot trust God to be faithful in relationship, we will find it impossible to trust mere man. We know man's frailties. It is only as we are confident of God's unending and full love that protects, heals, and guides us that we are able to risk loving others. We know man will fail, but God will NOT!

When confronted with lies, we must seek truth. We must investigate the facts and testimonies until all deception is exposed and only truth remains. The best way to know the truth about someone is to observe, listen, and talk **to them**. To know the truth about God will require spending time in His written testimony given by Himself, by friends who were with him every day for the three years of His earthly ministry, and by those who have been impacted by

Him. Read the accounts shared in Matthew, Mark, Luke, and John. Learn the truth as it comes directly from the Source...truth that has endured thousands of years of testing, challenges, and resistance. Ask the Holy Spirit to give you understanding. You will never see God the same way you did before.

I Know...

When I realized that I was trapped inside a web of lies that had crippled my ability to give and receive love from God and others, I became desperate for truth. I devoured the Word of God. I have filled countless journals with notes taken during study and times of prayer. I kept my heart open to correction and refused to resist change. I wanted freedom more than I wanted to be right. And I found it!

When I was a teenager, I was a habitual liar. I couldn't tell the truth about anything. It began when I tried to avoid angering or upsetting others and then grew into covering my mistakes. I told so many lies that, eventually, I began to believe them. It took me several years after salvation before I was comfortable giving my testimony. I was never sure if what I "remembered" truly happened or if it was one of the stories I made up in my mind. One lie led to another. Making the decision to receive truth was one of the most difficult decisions of my healing journey. I had to be willing to hear the truth about myself and accept blame for my choices; I had to be willing to see the truth about others, and release them from unfair judgments made against them. I had to be willing to learn the truth about God, though it meant that some of the most loved peers and teachers of my past had taught me some things incorrectly or added their opinion to God's pure commands. It was sometimes exhausting, often painful, and daily difficult—but it was worth it for the freedom truth brought to my life.

The remaining chapters of this book will walk you through the process of learning how to make healthy, godly choices that will bless your life. Many people want to start there, but until the trust issues are settled and a willingness to receive truth is established, it is a waste of time. We can't run from the healing process and be healed. We can't hurry it either.

Your way forward is simple. Ask the Holy Spirit to reveal truth to you about yourself, others, and God. As He shows you wrong perceptions, judgments and belief systems, turn from them (repent) and accept the truth. Your mind and emotions may still try to cling to the lies, but as you stay in God's Word and allow Him to renew your thinking, freedom will come. The Holy Spirit will help you let go of the old and receive the new. I promise!

It is time to begin YOUR quest for truth...

CHAPTER THREE

Choosing Truth

In an ancient fairy tale, a sorceress looks into a mirror and asks, "Mirror, mirror on the wall, who's the fairest of them all?" Her entire self-confidence and sense of beauty was determined by what she **saw** and **heard** in that mirror! If the report was positive, she was content. If the report seemed negative, however, she was outraged and distressed. In her frustration, she attempted to destroy the beauty of those around her. In the end, her vengeance resulted in her own destruction. What a tragic story!

Have you ever watched people when they stand near a mirror? All stop (even briefly) to catch a glimpse of themselves. When you watch their reaction, you learn much of what they think about themselves. Some smile broadly and primp – "Looking good!" their smiles say. Some frown; others walk away with, "What a bummer," written all over their faces. The astonishing truth is that many who seem comfortable with themselves are not necessarily beautiful by man's standards. Yet many who seem to reject their appearances are truly lovely. How can this be?

People determine what they see in the mirror, even before they look. Their self-perception is reflected in the glass. Women who have rejected themselves see only confirmation of their inadequacies and flaws. Men bound by self-hatred see proof of their failure and loathing. Both desperately need to see the TRUTH. They need to discover who they **really** are.

In John 14:6, Jesus said, "I am the Way, the TRUTH, and the Life." As we gaze into His eyes, we are finally able to see the true reflection of who we are.

"And you shall know the TRUTH and the TRUTH shall make you free..."

(John 8:32)

As we see ourselves through the eyes of Jesus, we see TRUTH. We see ourselves as He sees us, without the rejection, ridicule, or words of man. This truth enables us to shake off the lies of man and wholly embrace the life God has given to us. Man's words are slowly replaced with God's Word, and our minds are renewed!

We must come to see the truth about our identity if we are to be truly free. When our perception is altered, we often make faulty decisions that bring destruction to our lives and to those we love. If a woman believes that she deserves to be abused—that it is "her fault"—she may choose to remain in an abusive relationship. If someone believes that he is without hope and cannot change, he will often become depressed or even contemplate suicide. A child who believes she is stupid may not do well in school; her failure comes as the result of her lack of confidence rather than her lack of ability. A woman who believes she is unattractive may either "dress down" and avoid all relationships for fear of rejection OR attempt to transform herself through obsessive diets, clothing, or relationships. What we believe about ourselves impacts the decisions made every day; it's called the SELF-fulfilling prophecy.

For much of my life, my "mirror" was the opinion of others. I looked to significant family members, friends, and peers to "see" who I was. Their opinions of me became my own opinion. If they were critical of my appearance, I saw my reflection as flawed. If they had a negative opinion regarding my performance, I saw my reflection as that of a failure or disappointment. My self-esteem was extremely low, which caused me to make decisions that devalued and hindered me in life. Eventually, I had to allow God to take down and destroy the false images of self that the enemy portrayed through the opinions of others. It was the only way to be free! I had to consciously choose to look only to God for my reflection. When gazing into the Word of truth, I was able to see myself in truth. I saw the "me" God created me to be...a woman made in the image of God to bear His reflection in the earth.

Our wrong perceptions of self hurt others as well. A perfect example of this is found in Numbers 13 and 14. Ten Israelite spies returned from the land of Canaan with a negative report. By that evening, the entire camp of Israel moaned and complained with the ten. Their negativity and wrong self-perception was a poison that infected thousands of lives in one day.

"Then they told him, and said: 'We went to the land where you sent us. It truly flows with milk and honey, and this is its fruit. Nevertheless, the people who dwell in the land are strong; the cities are fortified and very large; moreover, we saw the descendants of Anak there...' Then Caleb quieted the people before Moses, and said, 'Let us go up at once and take possession, for we are well able to overcome it.'

But the men who had gone up with him said, 'We are not able to go up against the people, for they are stronger than we.'

And they gave the children of Israel a bad report of the land which they had spied out, saying, 'The land through which we have gone as spies is a land that devours its inhabitants, and all the people whom we saw in it are men of great stature. There we saw the giants...and we were like grasshoppers in our own sight, and so we were in their sight. So all the congregation lifted up their voices and cried and the people wept that night.'" (Taken from Numbers 13:27-14:1)

Too often, those hurt by our negative self-perception are the ones nearest and dearest to us—our children. Without realizing it, we infuse them with our low self-esteem and wrap them up in our bondage. I remember a woman that I knew long ago. She had a lovely smile, gentle voice, and was always kind to everyone. She had three children, and the oldest boy attended our youth group. One night she volunteered in the Youth Service and witnessed the boy entering the room. He was quiet and looked nervously at the growing crowd of young people. With his hands tucked in the pockets of his over-sized jacket, he made his way across the room and slumped into a chair. He observed the entire service and avoided any situations where he might be called upon to speak or participate in some way. His mother suddenly ran from the room in tears.

The mother wept as she said, "He is me!" She had long suffered from low self-esteem and struggled socially. We prayed together and the Lord reminded me of a scripture. I shared Genesis, chapter one with the precious woman, noting how God created everything to reproduce after its own kind. This is the natural law of reproduction— dogs reproduce dogs, the seed of the apple tree produces more apple trees, and so on. But there is a spiritual dynamic to this as well. Whatever we as parents and leaders allow in our lives will be naturally and spiritually reproduced in our children. In this case, the mother's wrong self-perception was reproduced in her son, though they had never discussed it. In fact, the mother had lavished encouragement on her son his entire life! Still, the law of reproduction could not be denied.

When the woman realized that her low self-esteem had transferred to her son, she determined to reverse the cycle. She began an all-out effort to change her perception of herself, renewing her mind with the Word of God. She had others praying for her, and she began to step out and try new things. She became increasingly vocal in social gatherings and participated more in church activities. She even got a new job! Though she never shared any of this with her son, he too began to change. As the changes progressed in her life, they began to flow into his life. The law of spiritual reproduction worked and the young man became an active member of the youth group before the year was ended. Our lives WILL impact the next generation.

It is time to learn the truth about ourselves!

We May Already Be Who Satan Says We Can't Be!

Remember the scriptures we read in Genesis 3 in the previous chapter? Satan, disguised as the serpent, insinuated to Eve that her eyes were NOT open; that she was NOT like God, and that she did NOT know good from evil. She was missing something! The enemy lied to her! Genesis 2:25 tells us that Adam and Eve's eyes were open and able to see their nakedness. Genesis 1:26 clearly states that they were created in the image of God. They were already LIKE God! In Genesis 3:3, they knew it was good to obey God and reject the forbidden fruit and that it was wrong (or evil) to disobey Him and eat the fruit. They already WERE who the serpent said they were not. They already had what the serpent said they didn't have. The opposite was true!

Satan's lies sound exactly the same today. He implies that we ARE NOT, HAVE NOT, and DON'T REALLY KNOW. From the beginning of time until this day, he has continuously bombarded mankind with self-doubt and negativity towards their self-perceptions and God. In most cases, we already are what Satan tells us we cannot be. We may not see it yet ourselves, but it is true. We often have what he tells us we cannot have – we just don't realize it yet! We already know what he claims we do not know, though we may not understand it.

My Testimony

School was never easy for me. I struggled socially because of missing too much school due to my father's illness or my own. At times, my sister and I had to live with relatives, taking schoolwork with us and missing weeks of school at a time. The school was cooperative, but the classmates were not. Insecurity caused by the neighbor's abuse and family's difficulties resulted in a great insecurity that impacted me academically. I froze when forced to recite information in front of the class or when taking a test. Math seemed a foreign language! No matter how hard I tried, the arithmetic problems seemed overwhelming. Years later, I discovered I had a "sequencing disability" that caused the numbers to get turned around in my head; but at the time, I had no idea. When negative words were added by family members or peers, I was sure of my stupidity. I was stupid. I decided I couldn't learn like others. I threw myself into the art and drama classes where I thought I could hide my inability to learn. By the time I entered the last few years of high school, I was far from God and hiding my insecurities in alcohol and the partying lifestyle. I gave up on learning.

After graduation, it was expected that I would go to college. Due to my lack of effort, my grades were very poor, and there were few options for financial aid. I wanted so much to please my parents and decided to go to a local community college. I decided to be a special education teacher. I truly had a heart for others and wanted to do something to help someone. My father was a teacher, and I decided I would be one too.

The first week of school, I went to—and enjoyed—every class. I found that I liked learning. I loved the books. Reading was my favorite pastime. I felt increasingly uncomfortable around the other students, however. They all seemed so smart! They had answers and weren't afraid to debate with the teachers. I was mostly silent, afraid that if I opened my mouth, everyone would know how stupid I really was. I was the invisible student until the end of the first week. When a teacher insisted I give a speech in front of the class, I became distraught and wasn't able to make it to the bathroom before vomiting. I was so embarrassed that I determined never to go back to class again.

This created a dilemma. I was afraid to tell my parents that I wasn't going to go to school anymore. I was ashamed to tell them how I failed. I was slowly finding my way to God, which wouldn't allow me to outright lie to them anymore. The only alternative seemed to be to get up in the morning and drive to the school as I told them I was doing. Then I would go into the cafeteria and read the books, studying on my own and ignoring the other students. I felt this wasn't "quite" a lie. I didn't know what else to do. I couldn't help that I was *too stupid* to go to school. I believed I could not learn. This plan worked well until grades were released; and my parents opened the mail before I could get to it. I wasn't welcome again at home for nearly a week. I didn't know how to explain my fear and shame to them.

Years went by, and eventually I realized that I COULD learn. I began to study God's Word and discovered a style of learning that worked for me. I gained confidence and began to use other study aids. Eventually, I found myself writing training manuals and studies used to help other people around the world. I was never stupid. Satan used circumstances in life and the negative words of man to convince me of a lie. Thank God for truth!!!

Recognize That Somebody Has Been Lying to You!

"Why do you not understand My speech? Because you are not able to listen to My Word. You are of your father the devil, and the desires of your father you want to do. He was a murderer from the beginning, and does not stand in the truth, because there is **no truth in him**. When he speaks a lie, he speaks from his own resources, for **he is a liar and the father of it**." (John 8:43-44)

Satan IS the father of all lies. There is no truth in Him. Whatever negative thoughts or feelings he brings to our minds are lies. He is the source of every lie we have heard or chosen to believe about ourselves.

Remember our beloved Peter? Peter spoke by revelation of the Holy Spirit and was acknowledged by Jesus.

"Simon Peter answered and said, 'You are the Christ, the Son of the living God.'" (Matthew 16:16)

Christ affirmed Peter's revelation, acknowledging his Divine revelation in front of his peers. It was a special moment of recognition for the big fisherman. Maybe the affirmation received here caused him to become a little bit proud, for a few verses later we find him quickly challenging the Words of Jesus. He seems to feel no hesitation in arguing with the Son of God!

"From that time, Jesus began to show to His disciples that He must go to Jerusalem, and suffer many things from the elders and chief priests and scribes, and be killed, and be raised the third day. Then Peter took Him aside and began to rebuke Him, saying, 'Far be it from You, Lord; this shall not happen to You!' But He turned and said to Peter, 'Get behind Me, Satan! You are an offense to Me, for you are not mindful of the things of God, but the things of men.'" (Matthew 16:21-23)

Jesus quickly realized that the challenge and negative words coming from the mouth of His friend were not from man, but from the devil himself. Though he loved Peter, He refused to accept the lies spoken through him. He put God's Word above man's. The beauty of His reaction is that He did not rebuke his friend; He rebuked the one speaking through His friend. He understood that Peter's love for Him combined with perhaps a bit of pride hindered his ability to hear the truth and allowed him to become a mouthpiece for the enemy. He didn't hate Peter for the offence. His relationship with Peter wasn't altered by the exchange. Jesus knew who His enemy was. Ephesians 6:12 states, "we do not wrestle with flesh and blood, but against principalities, against powers, against the rulers of the darkness of this age, against spiritual hosts of wickedness in the heavenly places."

We Have an Enemy!

It's so easy to forget this simple truth. We have AN enemy—one enemy. He is behind every hurt, rejection, neglect, abuse, and injustice we have ever experienced. He used people who were either lost and unknowingly slaves to him or ignorant believers who didn't understand. Either way, he was the source of it all. Getting angry and bitter at the person used by Satan is like getting angry at the lights in your house when the power goes out. It's not the light fixture's fault. Look to the power source!

When the devil voices an opinion about you through someone that opposes the Word of God, you must choose who you will believe. No one else can choose for you. God has given you the ability to choose who and what you will believe. Find out who God says you are. He is the One Who made you! God knows all about you, even better than you know yourself. He is the one who formed you in your mother's womb! He speaks only TRUTH. When you look into His Word, you will see a true reflection of your heart and soul.

"For You formed my inward parts; You covered me in my mother's womb. I will praise You, for I am fearfully and wonderfully made; Marvelous are Your works, and that my soul knows very well. My frame was not hidden from You, when I was made in secret, and skillfully wrought in the lowest parts of the earth. Your eyes saw my substance, being yet unformed. And in Your Book they all were written, the days fashioned for me, when as yet there were none of them." (Psalm 139:13-16)

It's Time for The REAL You to Be Known!

So…who DOES God say you are? Maybe it's just as important to know who you are NOT.

You are NOT an orphan.

You are NOT alone.

You are NOT rejected, unwanted, or unloved!

"For as many as are led by the Spirit of God, these are sons [children] of God. For you did not receive the spirit of bondage again to fear, but you received the Spirit of adoption by whom we cry out, 'Abba, Father.' The Spirit Himself bears witness with our spirit that we are children of God, and if children, then heirs—heirs of God and joint heirs with Christ, if indeed we suffer with Him, that we may also be glorified together." (Romans 8:14-17)

"But what does it say? 'The word is near you, in your mouth and in your heart' [that is the word of faith which we preach]: that if you confess with your mouth the Lord Jesus and believe in your heart that God has raised Him from the dead, you will be saved. For with the heart one believes unto righteousness, and with the mouth confession is made unto salvation. For the Scripture says, 'Whoever believes on Him will not be put to shame.'" (Romans 10:9-11)

"Blessed are those whose lawless deeds are forgiven, and whose sins are covered; Blessed is the man [woman] to whom the Lord shall not impute sin." (Romans 4:7-8)

"Or do you not know that your body is the temple of the Holy Spirit who is in you, whom you have from God, and you are not your own? For you were bought at a price; therefore, glorify God in your body and in your spirit, which are God's." (I Corinthians 6:19-20)

"Now He who establishes us with you in Christ and has anointed us is God, who also has sealed us and given us the Spirit in our hearts as a guarantee." (I Corinthians 12:20-21)

"Therefore, if anyone is in Christ, he [she] is a new creation; old things have passed away; behold all things have become new. Now all things are of God, who has reconciled us to Himself through Jesus Christ, and has given us the ministry of reconciliation." (2 Corinthians 5:17-18)

"Blessed be the God and Father of our Lord Jesus Christ, who has blessed us with every spiritual blessing in the heavenly places in Christ, just as He chose us in Him before the foundation of the world, that we should be holy and without blame before Him in love, having predestined us to adoption as sons [children] by Jesus Christ to Himself, according to the good pleasure of His will, to the praise of the glory of His grace, by which He made us accepted in the Beloved. In Him we have redemption through His blood, the forgiveness of sins, according to the riches of His grace, which He made to abound toward us in all wisdom and prudence, having made known to us the mystery of His will, according to His good pleasure which He purposed in Himself, that in the dispensation of the fullness of the times He might gather together in one all things in Christ, both which are in heaven and which are on earth—in Him. In Him also we have obtained an inheritance, being predestined according to the purpose of Him who works all things according to the counsel of His will, that we who first TRUSTED Christ should be to the praise of His glory. In Him you also TRUSTED, after you heard the word of truth, the gospel of your salvation; in whom also, having believed, you were sealed with the Holy Spirit of promise, who is the guarantee of our inheritance until the redemption of the purchased possession, to the praise of His glory." (Ephesians 1:3-14)

You ARE:

God's Handiwork

A Child of God

A Joint Heir with Christ

An Ambassador of Christ

A New Creation

A Carrier of His Spirit

Forgiven

Anointed

Reconciled to the Father

The Temple of the Holy Spirit

Purchased by God

Chosen by God

Planned by God

Without a doubt, God's view of you is better than your view of yourself. The good news is that your thinking can change! Your mind can be renewed through the Word of God. His Word can wash away the old patterns of thought and establish new. I challenge you to research the scriptures and find your true identity there. You are so much more

than you know! Hidden underneath the struggles, hurts, and

experiences of the past is an incredible prince or princess—a

child of the King!

CHAPTER FOUR

Choosing to Release Shame

I have a vivid memory from my childhood that stays with me today. My mother and I were in a small store, picking up a medical prescription for my father. I was perhaps nine or ten years old. My body grew fast that year, and I felt like a giraffe that lumbered along, tripping over my long legs and knocking things over with my arms. Sometimes the other children teased me about my long arms, reminding me that soon my hands would be dragging on the floor like a chimpanzee when I walked. To add to the look, my "grown-up" teeth grew in crooked, bringing more jeers from some classmates. I was self-conscious and tried to be invisible whenever possible!

One of my mother's friends approached us in the store that day. She greeted my mother warmly and asked about my father. Then my mother introduced me to her. The woman looked down and appeared shocked by my appearance. To this day, I have no idea why she looked at me that way. I immediately assumed that she was appalled by my long legs and "ape-like" arms or my crooked smile. Every negative word anyone had ever spoken concerning my appearance filled my mind. I moved behind my mother and stood as close as I could. I could no longer look the woman in the eye. I felt ashamed. The shame was so real and so deep that I can feel it still today, so many years later.

I didn't have to feel that way. I don't have to feel that shame today. *I can choose to let it go*. Webster's dictionary defines "shame" as "a painful emotion caused by consciousness of guilt, shortcoming, impropriety, or disgrace, dishonor, something that brings small regret, censure, or reproach." In other words, shame can be the result of my own behavior or mistake. It call also stem from a perceived shortcoming or from the experience of being dishonored by someone else. When shame enters a life, it immediately stunts spiritual, emotional, mental, and even physical growth. It is important for you and I to recognize and deal with shame issues in our lives so that the gospel will not be hindered in and through us.

Shame takes on many forms. It is the silent pain behind the outward struggle with sin or bondage. It is the root of self-destructiveness and the motivating force of perfectionism. It is the invisible cause of every positive effort's defeat. It is the voice of hopelessness and despair to every dream. It is the propelling force behind promiscuity and self-destructive habits. Shame punishes the person who wears it.

There is a vast difference between shame and guilt. Guilt speaks, "I did a bad thing!" while shame declares, "I AM a bad thing!" Guilt addresses the behavior. Shame accuses and attacks the identity of the believer. Like a worm that eats through the inner core of the apple, shame erodes the inner self. When a man or woman struggles with shame issues, they often feel as if they are empty and incomplete.

Guilt is a mobilizing force producing repentance and change. It is often inspired by the Holy Spirit as He convicts us of sin. However, He is never the Author of our shame. When God looks at us, He sees us through the blood of Jesus. He sees us pure and made holy by the blood of the Lamb. He sees us as in our new creation form, forgiven, cleansed and completely justified! Sadly, many of us still see ourselves as the old creation—the broken person we were before Christ. We need our thinking to be changed! We need to see ourselves the way God sees us!

The High Cost of Shame...

I remember the day God began dealing with the issue of shame in my life. I was sitting at home praying and telling God how much I loved Him. I heard His Voice say, "If you love me so much, why do you allow sin in your life?" I was stunned. I cried out, "What sin is left?" I had renounced and been set free from ungodly relationships, alcohol and drugs, and so much more. I couldn't imagine what was left! He didn't leave me guessing. In the next moment He said, "Your low self-esteem [shame] is sin." He then took me to the story of Israel in Numbers 13:32-14:9.

The Israelites had been legally freed from all bondage. But the years of abusive words and treatment continued to shape their views of themselves. Thus, they were intimidated by the unknown and the greatness of the enemy. Their shame told them they were nothing but grasshoppers, easily crushed and broken. They were unable to see the truth of who they were. They were unable to see their *incredible* potential. When the inner voice of shame contradicted the Voice of God, they chose to obey shame. This made shame their lord and master. This was the sin they suffered for.

Whatever dictates our decisions is our lord. No matter where the shame in our lives came from, it is our choice to obey it or not. We can choose to bring shame into submission to the lordship of Jesus Christ.

If you have received Christ as your Lord and Savior, you are LEGALLY pardoned of all previous wrongdoing, forgiven, loved, cleansed, and made into a new creation in Him! The truth is, you have already been set free from shame. Without realizing it, you've been choosing to remain in the past and accept the shame that no longer belongs to you. It's time for you to experience the genuine freedom Jesus purchased for you.

There are three major sources for shame in a believer's life: Satan, our sin, and the sin of others.

1) **Satan.** As the enemy of our souls, he attempts to hinder our spiritual growth by condemning us for our sin or mistakes.

When we receive the condemnation of the enemy rather than the forgiveness offered by Christ, we limit our ability to partake of God's kingdom. We are nagged by overwhelming thoughts of hopelessness, failure, and memories of the past. We are not challenged or changed by the condemnation. Often we find ourselves running from the only One Who can set us free.

Overcoming the accusations and condemnation of the enemy requires repentance, cleansing, and spiritual warfare. All three elements are needed to attain wholeness. We must begin by owning the fact that we have been bowing to the enemy's lies and allowing his condemnation to "lord" over us. Whatever we allow to dictate our lives IS our lord! The Bible declares that we are to have no other Lord but Jesus, making our submission to Satan's lies a sin. Thus we repent (ask forgiveness and turn away from) the accusations and condemnation, renouncing their control over our thoughts, speech, and behaviors. This is the beginning of wholeness.

However, it's also the place where many of us refuse to go on.

There is a tendency in us to perceive ourselves as victims. We tell ourselves and others that we can't change the way we are or the things we do because we've been hurt. Our past binds us. We blame our struggles on the people who wounded us. The thought of US repenting for any of our issues seems wrong! It's their fault! Self-pity paralyzes us, and we stubbornly refuse to own any of the responsibility for our problems. No matter who did what to us, WE choose every single day whether we will allow the experience to rule our lives OR if we will follow the Holy Spirit into a life of freedom. Accepting the fact that we have chosen to bow to shame, allowing it to control our thoughts, lives, and decisions, is essential.

The people who wronged us could come crawling to us tomorrow, beg for our forgiveness, and do everything possible to make things right, and we would STILL struggle with shame. They may have brought the shame into our lives through abuse, neglect, or negativity; but we are the ones now holding it close and giving it control of our lives. This is why repentance is necessary. We must realize that we have a choice to make.

Repentance is simply turning in the opposite direction, choosing to turn away from something we've been doing, saying, or being. When we repent of allowing shame to control our lives, we're simply stating our determination to reject shame's power over us and begin living free of it!

When we repent, there is a supernatural cleansing that takes place. I John 1:9 promises that as we repent, God forgives us completely and then divinely washes away all sin—anyplace in our hearts, minds, or behaviors where we have been "missing the mark." We are supernaturally cleansed of all shame. He cleanses us in a way that man never can. True freedom can only come in His cleansing flow.

Once we have experienced this Divine cleansing, we will still need to retrain our brains! Our minds have been conditioned to think *shame* thoughts. Shame has become a habit and way of life to us. Renewal of our minds begins with the Bible. As we begin to saturate our lives with the Word of God, the Word of God becomes a strong astringent that washes away the crooked ways of thought, speech, and behavior developed by the previous sin. As we read, study, meditate on, and listen to God's Word, our minds are renewed.

When this process is complete, we stand knowing we are confident and clean before God. There is absolutely nothing else we need to do to be "right" in His sight. It is as if there were never a negative thought in our mind. It is forgotten. We finally believe that God sees only blood-washed, Word-washed children that He loves more than life.

This is When the Fun REALLY Begins!

Just when you are experiencing the wonderful freedom found in Jesus, the enemy may strike. He understands that your new understanding of redemption is shutting a door to him. No longer will Satan be able to control you through shame-filled thoughts, words, or issues. As you live as the new creation you are, the adversary is robbed of power to afflict or tempt you. To make matters worse, you are probably spreading your newfound freedom to everyone you know! You've become "Enemy #1" to the powers of darkness! This is why you may suddenly experience spiritual warfare shortly after your life-changing breakthrough.

The enemy is weak and vulnerable to God's power and bidding, but he is not stupid. He knows that if he can convince us that we are still accused and condemned before God, then we will open the gate for the deception to return to "lord" our lives. He begins to bombard our minds with doubt. Circumstances occur that make it appear as if we were not set free. He speaks through unwitting individuals to remind us of our mistakes. If we do not understand that this is spiritual warfare, we will open the door to the enemy and find ourselves in greater bondage to his lies than before.

The Bible is called the "Sword of the Spirit." It is at this point we must grab the "Sword" and use it as a weapon against the adversary. We must put the Word that we have read, studied, meditated on, and listened to into our mouths. We must speak the truth of God's Word in our prayers and against every doubt, negative thought, and attack of the evil one. If we refuse to bow to the enemy's accusations and condemnation, his lies will have no power to control our lives. We will not only BE free...we will STAY free!

Write a prayer in the space below, repenting of times you have believed and bowed to Satan's lies and accusations against you. Choose to no longer bow! Ask God for His grace to turn away from these negative belief systems forever.

Receive His forgiveness and supernatural cleansing. Then follow the guidelines shared in the previous paragraphs to renew your mind. It is God's will and delight to set you free.

If you are a Christian and have taken authority over the enemy, he must submit to you. Therefore, if you continue to struggle with shame, there may be other reasons. Perhaps YOU are now the one opening the gate for shame to enter your heart and mind. This leads us to the second cause of shame:

2) **Sin**. Shame also enters our lives when we choose to sin.

In Genesis 2:25, God created man free of shame. Both the man and woman enjoyed a freedom that only infants now know—the freedom of never having disobeyed God. This freedom produced a liberty in the first couple that allowed them to be comfortable even when most exposed to one another. They accepted their bodies with confidence. They were able to be totally honest with each other. They feared nothing and had nothing to hide. They found it easy to stand before the Creator uncovered and bare. They found it easy to walk near Him. This was what God intended for mankind from the beginning.

In Genesis 3:7-10, everything changes. The couple commits the first act of disobedience to God and sins against Him. This act opens the door to a shame they had never experienced before. Suddenly, they are unable to look at one another comfortably. They feel awkward and try to hide their bodies. Later, they try to hide from God. Nothing is the same anymore. They have lost confidence, inner peace, and that wonderful comfortable feeling they once had with God and one another. The shame that now enters their life comes because of their decision to disobey God. The serpent may have suggested sin, but they CHOSE. Their sin opened the gate to so much pain and suffering.

I Understand Their Problem...

Before dedicating my life to Christ as an 18-year-old young woman, I lived far from God. In complete rebellion, I partied with friends and lived a promiscuous lifestyle. After my salvation, I slowly pulled away from unhealthy friendships and became depressed. God's Word eventually altered my lifestyle, and I took a break from dating so that I could pursue Jesus.

I met my husband months later after visiting the Christian Coffeehouse (Street Ministry) that he directed. We were married less than a year later, and I moved into the Coffeehouse with him to help minister to the various street people and addicts that came to our door. It was an interesting way to start a marriage!

I loved my husband so much, but I lied to him. When we first began dating, I told him about the abuse I had experienced but failed to tell him about my promiscuity. I didn't want to lose him. I was so ashamed of my sin. I still saw myself as damaged goods. So I hid the truth from him, and we married with the lie between us.

One day, a man came into the coffeehouse. I barely recognized him. Most of the men I had "known" before Jesus were met at bars and parties. We were intoxicated and would likely never see one another again. The man's car had broken down, and he needed to use our phone. My husband told him where the phone was, and he turned to see me; I was sitting in the kitchen. The man's eyes grew wide, and he blurted out, "What's a slut like you doing in a place like this?" My face flamed red, and I broke out in a sweat. I felt sick to my stomach. Shame felt like a heavy brick on my heart. I couldn't even look at my poor husband. Instead, I just handed the man the phone and walked away.

All night long I waited for my husband to mention the incident, but he never did. Years went by before we ever discussed it. I guess he knew I wasn't ready to face it yet. The shame weighed on my heart, and it took me many years to finally confess the truth and receive the freedom Christ had so generously given me at the cross. My lie had allowed shame to become a constant companion for far too long. We weren't created to carry shame!

Psalm 139 states that we were created by God, woven together by His hands in our mother's womb. In this creation, there was no shame or reproach. It was never God's intention that we be ashamed of our bodies, actions, or inner self. He made us in His image to reflect His glory! It is so important for us to understand this truth. If God had intended for you and I to live with shame, He would have created us with it from the beginning! Instead, He created us with a purity and confidence that reflects Him.

"If we confess our sins, He is faithful and just to forgive us our sins and to cleanse us from all unrighteousness."

(I John 1:9)

Again, this scripture promises that when we confess our sins, Christ forgives us! Confession brings release from all guilt and shame. It enables us to experience God's forgiveness. When He forgives us, He also cleanses us from ALL unrighteousness. When we believe this and allow Him to wash away the sin—when we truly accept the sin as forgiven—we are free of shame!

This scripture is often used to bring the lost to Christ, but it was actually written to the believers of the early church. God knew that His people would need forgiveness even after salvation. It is no surprise to Him! This should give us confidence in approaching Him for the forgiveness and cleansing we need. Whether the door that opened to shame was sin in the past or present, it is shut the same way. Confession of sin leads to cleansing and the gate is closed to shame.

Take a moment to confess your sin right now, in the box below. Choose to believe I John 1:9. Accept God's forgiveness and cleansing of your heart and mind. Let the shame be washed away with the sin as your receive a revelation of His mercy and grace.

Sometimes the source of shame is much more difficult to deal with. We can repent for allowing shame to control us. We can rebuke Satan. We can repent of our sin. But when the sin is committed by others against us, resulting in the struggle with shame, it can be much harder to face. This is the third cause of shame.

3) **The Sin of Others.** Shame is sometimes the result of sin committed against us. It has nothing to do with our behavior. It is a choice made by someone else to sin against us.

"Now when she had brought them to him to eat, he took hold of her and said to her, 'Come, lie with me, my sister.' But she answered him, 'No, my brother, do not force me, for no such thing should be done in Israel. Do not do this disgraceful thing! And I, where could I take my shame? And as for you, you would be like one of the fools in Israel. Now therefore, please speak to the king; for he will not withhold me from you.' However, he would not heed her voice; and being stronger than she, he forced her and lay with her." (2 Samuel 13:11-14)

The situation outlined in 2 Samuel 13 is a perfect example of this truth. Amnon sinned against his sister. Tamar was innocent before man and God. She was obedient to her father. She resisted sin. She fought it! Yet in the end, Amnon overcame her will and sinned against her body. He used her. He abused her. Afterwards, he added to her shame by rejecting her completely.

I've often pondered on Tamar's life. My heart aches for the young woman who lost her sense of innocence and identity. Her future was altered forever because of her brother's sin. No one defended her. Instead of encouraging her to put the situation behind her and continue to embrace life, she was isolated and put aside. Perhaps her presence reminded her family of its imperfections. No one but God knows for sure. But in the end, she became a recluse who never knew the joy of godly relationship or intimacy. Shame locked her in her house and prevented her from embracing life.

Why did Tamar allow herself to be locked away? Why did she live the rest of her days in mourning? Why didn't she put it behind her and go on with life? Though her family encouraged her isolation, she could have chosen to escape it.

I think Tamar lost more than her innocence in Amnon's sin. *She lost her ability to choose.* Amnon took away her ability to choose when he forced his wishes upon her. He didn't ask her what she wanted. He didn't listen to her decision to abstain. He forced his choice and robbed her of her own. Something was broken inside the young girl, and she seemed unable to choose for herself from that day forward.

My Testimony

The rebellion I mentioned earlier was rooted in an experience much like Tamars. The abuse I experienced as a child impacted me in many ways. My low self-worth caused me to make poor decisions, often putting myself at unnecessary risk. One poor decision led me to a small party at a friend's home. The mother was gone, and the father was partying with drugs and alcohol. As the others made their way to bedrooms and dark corners, I decided it was time to leave. I was shocked when the father put my keys down his pants and challenged me to get them. Grabbing hold of me, he began to force his touch and kisses. He was bigger than me and had his way. No pleading would stop him.

Early the next morning, I cleaned myself up and drove home, sore and filled with shame. I buried the incident in my heart. I cried and became angry with God. I looked for someone to blame. In truth, I blamed myself. I believed I was "damaged goods" and deserved whatever happened to me. No matter what I did, the memory remained, and shame found a near-permanent residence in my life.

My value of self was finally broken than day. There had been inklings of confidence in me before, but no more. I began to party and gave myself away. It didn't seem to matter anymore. I stayed in unhealthy relationships. I let other people make decisions for me. I threw caution to the wind. I thought I had lost my ability to choose.

That all changed when I gave my life to Jesus. He restored my ability to choose. He cleansed me of the shame of this man's sin against me, as well as all the sin I had committed before and after that awful night. He made me new! He renewed my innocence before Him. He restored my confidence. He gave me strength to make decisions again. No more allowing life, bondage, or others to choose for me.

A Father's Sin...

"Then Saul's anger was aroused against Jonathon, and he said to him, 'You son of a perverse, rebellious woman! Do I not know that you have chosen the son of Jesse to your own shame and to the shame of your mother's nakedness? For as long as the son of Jesse lives on the earth, you shall not be established, nor your kingdom. Now therefore, send and bring him to me, for he shall surely die.' And Jonathon answered Saul his father, and said to him, 'Why should he be killed? What has he done?' Then Saul cast a spear at him to kill him, by which Jonathon knew that it was determined by his father to kill David. So Jonathon arose from the table in fierce anger, and ate no food the second day of the month, for he was grieved for David, because his father had treated him shamefully." (I Samuel 20:30-34)

Jonathon loved his father despite his shortcomings. In this story, he was shocked by his father's unfair treatment of a friend. When Jonathon attempted to defend his friend, his father raged at him in front of the crowd gathered for the banquet. He called him names, spoke words of defeat and death over his life and destiny, and finally struck out in his anger, nearly killing Jonathon. None of this was Jonathon's fault. He had done nothing wrong. Still he was left grieving, angry, and unable to eat. His father's choices impacted his life whether he deserved it or not. He was shamed that day by his father's words and anger. Their relationship was never the same.

Jonathon didn't get to choose whether he was publically shamed or not that day. King Saul took the power of choice away from him with his abusive anger. Jonathon eventually fulfilled the negative prophecies his father shouted at him, dying by his side on the battlefield. It is a sad story, but it could have ended much differently.

Have you ever wondered why Jonathon remained with King Saul? At that time in history, it wasn't uncommon for a son to join forces against his own father for a kingdom's cause. He knew David was God's choice as king. He could have chosen to walk away and end his father's abuse, especially since this was the second time Saul was willing to kill Jonathon. He could have continued to love and pray for his father while joining forces with David. Instead, he stayed loyal to his abuser as so many do today. He stayed at his beck and call, though it led to his death.

I believe Jonathon stayed with Saul for the same reason many remain in unhealthy relationships today. They think they have lost their ability to choose and allow the abusers in their lives to make decisions for them. They simply exist. They have no will of their own. They accept their situation in life and endure it bravely—never realizing that they have the power to walk away.

I am not recommending that you leave your spouse after a nasty argument. I am not saying it is wrong to remain in a relationship with an angry person...but there needs to be definite boundaries placed around every relationship. No person has the right to choose for you. You have the right to decide what you will do, who you will be, and what you will tolerate. As a believer in Jesus, your decisions are guided by the wisdom and counsel of the Holy Spirit so that you are sure to succeed; but no man has the right to choose for you. When man violates your right to choose, it is time to establish clear boundaries of relationship with planned consequences if the boundaries are ignored. If someone repeatedly violates the boundaries, it may be necessary to distance from them. This does not mean that you hate them or that you are punishing them; you are simply reclaiming your right to choose. God gave you that right. Fight for it!

To establish healthy boundaries in a relationship requires prayer and personal evaluation. What does that person do that shames or injures you? These words or behaviors become boundaries. They are the "No

Trespassing" signs of your life in all relationships. What will you do if that person violates these boundaries? Will you distance yourself from the relationship, refuse their phone calls, limit time spent with them? These consequences become the "Trespassers will be Prosecuted" warnings that surround your life. They protect you from being violated by others. They guard your right to choose.

What boundaries and consequences do you need to establish?

"Surely He has borne our griefs and carried our sorrows; yet we esteemed Him stricken, smitten by God and afflicted. But He was wounded for our transgressions, He was bruised for our iniquities; the chastisement for our peace was upon Him, and by His stripes we are healed." (Isaiah 53:4-5)

While attending a youth service at an Assembly of God church shortly after my salvation, I had an unusual experience. The pastor was displaying a picture of Christ's trial before crucifixion. Jesus was standing wearily with hands bound before his accusers. Suddenly, the picture came to life for me. I saw the soldiers rip the clothes from his body, exposing him and mocking his nakedness as they beat him with rods and fists. He was shamed as I had once been, and I felt His pain. Better yet, I knew He felt MY pain. I understood that Christ took the shame of abuse with him to the cross so I would not have to live under shame's dominion. I found a new level of peace in this revelation of truth. I didn't have to carry the shame of my sin, other's sin against me, or Satan's lies anymore.

Jesus endured shame for us at His crucifixion. If we believe what the Bible says, then Jesus already endured (carried, lifted away, bore up) our shame and sorrow so we wouldn't have to. We can refuse to carry it. We can lay it at the cross. We have the ability to refuse it. His shed blood was enough to set us free from our sin, their sin, and Satan's lies!

To continue carrying shame in our lives is to deny the power and beauty of Christ's sacrifice on the cross. He endured that cross (Hebrews 12:1-2) for the joy of seeing us free. We were the reason He allowed Himself to be murdered in such a way. He took all of our sin, iniquity, and shame with Him to the cross. It died with Him. It was buried with Him...*but it did not resurrect with Him*! When we identify with Christ as Lord and Savior, we identify with this death and resurrection. Our sin, iniquity, and shame are dead, and we are living free! Can you believe this?

"Do not fear, for you will not be ashamed; neither be disgraced, for you will not be put to shame; for you will forget the shame of your youth, and will not remember the reproach of your widowhood anymore For your Maker is your husband, the Lord of hosts is His name; and your Redeemer is the Holy One of Israel; He is called the God of the whole earth." (Isaiah 54:4-5)

Too many people allow the wounds of life—the shame and mistakes of the past—to rule their decisions. Their painful past and the abusers of life own and possess them. This does not have to be! In Jesus, we receive a new "Husband"—a new *Owner*, *Master*, and *Possessor*. We receive His life and the renewed ability to choose. In this scripture He promises that He will not leave us feeling dry, disappointed, shamed, injured or confused. He promises that

127

with Him, we can forget the shame of our youth or abandonment. We can enjoy newness of life!

The shame of the past does not have to control, own, or possess our lives as believers. God's intention continues to be freedom for His people. His only plans for your life are to do you GOOD and NOT evil all the days of your life (Jeremiah 29:11). You can trust Him. Let Him restore your ability to choose today.

CHAPTER FIVE

Choosing to Release Anger

Anger is a deceptive emotion. It is often a mask worn to hide other, less popular emotions such as hurt or fear. Anger is equated with strength and seen as the normal response to offence, injury, insult, or abuse. When you are angry, you can almost always find someone else to be angry with you. Anger is expected and accepted by society and is therefore a safe place to hide other emotions that are seen as weaknesses. The hidden issues then become the "fuel" for the "fire" that burns. The heat is intensified with new situations, causing hurt or fear. Eventually, you may begin to adopt other people's offences to give you more opportunity to vent the pent-up emotion. If not properly handled, the anger will eventually spiral out of control and bring pain to you and those you love.

There have been times in my marriage when I have exploded in anger at my husband, blaming him for the frustration I felt, only to dissolve in tears when the anger subsided. There was a hidden issue of my heart that fueled my passion and made the issue between us bigger than it was. This caused a strain on our relationship that impacted our children and ministry as well. Change came when I finally addressed the source of the anger and refused to use it to vent the real pain I was feeling inside. Change always follows on the heels of TRUTH.

An Angry Mask...

As you trail the life of King Saul in I Samuel, chapters 13-15, you find he was a great deceiver. He had a fierce anger that often resulted in bad choices that produced negative consequences in his life and family. His unrestrained anger caused him to hurl insults, false accusations, and threats against family and friends. At times, the anger would drive him to attempt bodily harm to others, seeking to kill David in his bed or to pierce him or Jonathon to the wall with a spear. He was consumed with his anger and did all he could to appease it. He determined that if only David was destroyed, he would be able to find peace. He herded his army to mountains, caves, and valleys, away from their homes and loved ones, to pursue David. But it didn't help appease his rage.

Nothing COULD help, because anger was not the real problem for Saul. The true source of his frustration came from deep within himself. His own failure to love God as David did; his own fear of man and fear of failure; his own low self-esteem …these rooted his rage. In the end, Saul's failure to deal with the true issues of his heart drove him to madness, a tormenting "spirit" from the Lord. I believe the "tormenting spirit" was simply the conviction of the Holy Spirit seeking to deal with these hidden issues. Refusal to respond to Him ended in a distress that could only be lifted when he was saturated in the love and Presence of God found in worship.

Many times Christians attempt to deal with excessive anger problems from the outside. They try to learn new coping mechanisms to help them discipline the outward reaction of their anger. But the truth is that they are still "wired" to the source of the anger and therefore eventually explode with it once again. It is like a lamp that is plugged into an electric socket in the home. If left plugged in, anyone can tamper with the lamp and set it on or off. The only way to keep the lamp "off" is to unplug it from the source of energy. The same is true of anger.

My Testimony

I had a million excuses for my anger problem. I blamed it on the abuse that I experienced, wounds from family members or friends, and injustice on the job, in church, or in society. I blamed my anger on lack of sleep or privacy, health issues, and lack of finances. The list was endless. Yet slowly my reasons were swept away as God healed the impact of the abuse and wounds, vindicated me of unjust judgments and situations, gave me the opportunity to stand for justice in the nations, taught me how to rest and spend time alone with Him, healed my body, and began to prosper our family. Suddenly, I had no one to blame...but me! Even then I seemed to find it easier to blame God. There must be something God still hadn't done for me!

Over the years, I became an expert at "holding the anger in" for seasons, and then hearing myself explode when I could no longer control it. When it exploded, my anger manifested as verbal attacks that were intense with emotion, and at times, accompanied by physical hitting or throwing of objects. I can well remember a day early in my marriage when I began shouting at my husband, hitting him on his chest while shouting, "C'mon, you wimp—fight like a man!" I wanted him to hit me back...but that's another story.

Needless to say, when my emotional outburst was finished, I was usually exhausted, weeping, and filled with shame and regret.

Unconsciously, I used anger as a means of control. I frightened away those I feared with my anger. I manipulated others with anger to get things done. My anger issues led to a controlling spirit that alienated relationships and hurt my witness for Christ. Beneath it all, I was afraid. I was afraid my husband would leave me, so I pushed him to see if he would run before I could risk trusting him. I was afraid of failing, so I pushed everyone on my team or family to work harder so that we would succeed. The more vulnerable I felt, the shorter my fuse and the more expressive my temper. It was a horrible cycle. I hated it; but I didn't know how to make it stop.

As I owned my anger issues and began to repent of the way I vented these emotions (hurting others), things began to change. I gave myself no excuse for expressing my anger in a way that hurt or controlled others. For a while, it felt as if I were apologizing to someone every five minutes! There were many times I wanted to justify the angry response and ignore the nudge of the Holy Spirit to make things right. But each time that I obeyed and yielded to His conviction, I felt lighter. It was as if I could finally breathe. The next step was praying until God revealed the source of my anger problem: the fear that hid behind it. As I allowed Him to heal these hidden issues, the anger seemed to disappear. Instead, I began to feel and share a grace toward others that made it easy to love and be loved. Relationships began to heal, and I experienced a surge of hope. It was wonderful!

Anger is Not a Sin!

Anger is a normal, God-created emotion. It is not evil. It is nothing to be ashamed of. The Bible does not say that we can never be angry. Instead, the Word of God teaches us what we should do *when* we are angry. Anger is not a sin. It is an emotion God feels and expresses. We were made in His image and therefore have an ability to feel this same anger. Godly anger may manifest in strong emotion or sentiment and can be a great motivator for bringing change. Let me give you an example...

A woman is in an abusive relationship. Every day her husband uses drugs and gets drunk before coming home, spending all of their finances on his addiction. If she asks him for anything or challenges him about his behavior, he releases a verbal onslaught that humiliates her. At times, he strikes out and leaves bruises on her face and body. Her greatest fear is what he might one day do to the children. Yet she stays. She continues to take the abuse day after day for many years. She finds many reasons for staying, despite the counsel of friends. Then one day, her husband strikes one of the children and the woman gets *angry*. She tells him she will not tolerate any more. She sets boundaries in the relationship and insists that he get help or leave. Never again does she allow him to hurt her. In this case, anger was a godly emotion that motivated the woman to make a positive change in her life.

When we have been abused in any way, it is normal to feel anger. Sometimes the shame speaks so loud that we are unable to hear it in our hearts for years. Sometimes the abusive situation results in a coping mechanism of numbness that will not allow us to feel the emotion. But eventually, the anger surfaces and must be dealt with. This is why we may find ourselves angry years after an offence, or even after the offender has died. Our anger in these cases is absolutely justified and even godly in response. What they did was wrong! They had no right to do it. If we are still in an abusive relationship or situation, the anger will usually motivate us to make a positive change. The anger can be a positive force in our lives.

A Real Man...

I Samuel 25:2-42 is an interesting story. David is remembered as a lover of God. At times, he can appear a saint in church history. Yet, he was simply a man. He DID love God. He WAS a worshipper. He DID have a heart after God's. AND, he was also wounded.

David had experienced rejection from his father who left him in the field, tending sheep during a once-in-a-lifetime feast with the Prophet Samuel. He had experienced belittling and rejection from his brothers on the field of battle. He had been falsely accused and pursued by a king he sought only to love and serve. He had lost security, home, and friends because of the pursuit. He was forced to hide like an animal in caves. King Saul made efforts to kill him more than once. In each of these situations, David outwardly responded, as we would expect him to—with godly restraint, pure heart, and faith towards God.

That is what makes this Scripture so hard to believe! David asks Nabal for food for his small flock of warriors after having protected Nabal's fields and herds from thieves. Nabal sees David through the eyes of Saul and refuses to help him. This is the first time Nabal offends David—and it proves to be his last. David is enraged by Nabal's refusal and determines to kill him, his family and servants, and to destroy his home. If it were not for the wise intervention of Nabal's wife, Abigail, he would have done it. He had no intention of restraining his anger this time. Why was it so different this time? Where is our David of godly restraint and pure heart? He has suddenly become a raging murderer!

Perhaps David felt the past rejection, false accusations and abuse more than he showed before this day. Could it be that he hid his hurt, confusion, and anger in his heart? Maybe he hid it because he wanted so much to please God. When you read the Songs written in his years of fleeing Saul, he expresses an emotion not readily seen in his behavior. Regardless, the anger was there, and was justified in his anger. He had every right to feel anger when treated this way. The anger was not wrong UNTIL it was expressed in a way that could have wounded others. This made his anger sin. David quickly repented and brought his anger under submission to God, giving the story a happy ending.

The Bible acknowledges that there will be times when we are angry...

"Be angry and do not sin: do not let the sun go down on your wrath, nor give place to the devil. Let him who stole steal no longer, working with his hands what is good, that he may have something to give him who has need. Let no corrupt word proceed out of your mouth, but what is good for necessary edification that it may impart grace to the hearers. And do not grieve the Holy Spirit of God by whom you were sealed for the day of redemption. Let all bitterness, wrath, anger, clamor, and evil speaking be put away from you, with all malice. And be kind to one another, tenderhearted, forgiving one another, even as God in Christ forgave you." (Ephesians 4:26-32)

WHEN we are angry, we are not to sin. The Bible does not forbid anger; it simply sets boundaries around it so that we can deal with it in positive ways. Simple direction is provided in this passage: let the anger go before going to bed at night. Set a time limit on how long you will allow yourself to be angry about the issue. Know when it is time to let it go. Staying angry won't change anything; won't help the situation. It will only allow the enemy a foothold in your mind, heart, and relationships.

The important issue is not whether or not we should get angry, but rather, what we will do with the anger we feel. King Saul's anger caused him to strike out at others when the true source of his frustration was himself. My anger caused me to strike out at others and myself, driving me into unhealthy relationships and behaviors that would sufficiently punish me for my "failures." I hit my husband, who was bigger than me, in the secret hope of his hitting me back. I have known others who could hold a "grudge" (anger and bitterness) for years, never realizing they were the only ones being truly hurt by it.

The High Cost of Unrestrained Anger...

Genesis 4:1-8 is a sad story that is repeated in families still today. The older brother is angry because his offering to God was not received. Instead of seeking God about why it was not received and making a change in what was offered, Cain found it easier to blame Abel. It was Abel's fault that Cain was angry. He took Abel to a field, perhaps to talk or argue. We will never know his plan. We can only know that sometime in the course of their walk together, Cain struck Abel in anger and killed him. We will never know if it were intentional or a horrible mistake. Ultimately, Cain carried the consequence of this moment of unrestrained anger for the rest of his life.

When Cain first became angry, God tried to warn him. The words used to describe Cain's anger translate to mean that he became *red with rage*, gritting his teeth, and breathing hard. God warned him that he must control his anger or be controlled by it. Cain had a choice. He could have asked God for help, and responded rightly to the emotion. Instead, he allowed his feelings to lead him. Anger leaves a trail of destruction when it is allowed to lead.

When our anger causes us to hurt ourselves or someone else, it becomes sin. It is no longer healthy or usable. It is a destroying fire. When we have allowed our anger to control our words, behaviors, thoughts, and decisions, we have made it "lord" of our lives. We have relinquished our ability to choose to an excessive emotion. There is only one way to deal with sin: we must repent. No matter where the anger originated, it is ours to deal with. No matter who did what to us, we must decide what we will do with the anger. This is why God gave us the power to choose...so that we could choose to release the anger that would hurt us and those we love.

Protecting the Temple

"Do you not know that you are the temple of God and that the Spirit of God dwells in you?" ... "Or do you not know that your body is the temple of the Holy Spirit who is in you, whom you have from God and you are not your own?"... "You were bought at a price; do not become slaves of men." (I Corinthians 3:16; 6:19; 7:23)

Very few people would allow someone to enter a church and begin tearing it apart. As soon as the person began to break the windows, throw the chairs, or knock over the pulpit, most people would intervene to stop them. They would know that it was wrong for the person to abuse the house of God.

Our bodies are the "temples" (houses) of the Holy Spirit, purchased by the shed blood of Jesus. We belong to

Him! Just as it is wrong for someone to abuse the church building when angry, it is equally as wrong for us to abuse our bodies—or others'—when angry. When we abuse others or ourselves in anger, we are abusing God. He lives within us by His Spirit. He feels every blow.

If our anger causes us to hurt ourselves or someone else, it is sin. Many people controlled by anger begin to develop destructive habits such as eating disorders, drug and/or alcohol addiction, pornography, abusive relationships, or self-inflicted wounds (cutting or burning one's self, excessive recklessness, suicidal thoughts or tendencies). This is never the will of God. He wants us to choose to release our anger to Him.

The beauty of salvation is that it restores our ability to choose. We no longer have to live under the dominion/control of the past, present, or future. We do not have to live in submission to self-destructive habits, self-condemnation, or excessive emotion. Memories do not have to control us. Because of what Jesus did for us at the cross (Isaiah 53), we are able to repent and turn away from the issues that once held us in bondage. We can choose to let go of our anger; to give it to God. We can decide to step past the issues that angered us and move on with our lives.

In I John 1:9, the scripture tells us to confess our sin. We must begin by admitting to ourselves and to God that we have sinned by allowing anger to control us. Then we must receive God's forgiveness (discussed at length in the next chapter) and allow Him to supernaturally cleanse us of the anger. This is followed with the renewing of our minds, thoughts, and behaviors with the Word of God. The Scriptures chip away at the old angry patterns and replace them with new, life-giving ways. Our entire way of thinking and responding to offences in life can be changed!

Best of all, we do not have to carry the regret or condemnation for our unrestrained anger with us into the future. We do not have to be ashamed of the times our angry outbursts hurt others or us. We do not have to feel awkward in God's Presence because we once raged against Him. All is forgiven the moment we choose to repent. He cleanses us of ALL of it. There is no need for us to be punished, for the mistakes have been erased.

How do we give our anger to God? Though we may want it to be gone in a moment, we will deal with it issue-by-issue, day-by-day. As a source of anger is revealed, we will need to open the door for God to bring His truth, healing, and love to us. In order for us to change the previous negative patterns, we will need patient continuance in God's Word. Renewal is a process. It took years for us to learn our ways of responding to anger; it will take time for us to learn new ways. There will be new offences along the way as well. The key is never to deny the anger; don't "stuff it" inside or pretend it is not there. Acknowledge it, confess it, and allow God to take it. You are on the path to wholeness.

CHAPTER SIX

Choosing to Release Fear

"...The thing that hath been, it is that which shall be and that which is done is that which shall be done: and there is no new thing under the sun."

(Ecclesiastes 1:9/KJV)

When I was less than six years old, my mother was working as a nurse's aid at a nearby hospital. My father had been very ill and was watching me at home. I wanted to play outside, so I put on my coat and ran out the door. I was playing on the swing set in our backyard and decided to go down the slide. As I began to slide, my hood hooked on the handrail and stopped me. I was hanging by my hood, flat on my back. I was so bundled and slippery that I couldn't seem to get foot leverage to move. I tried pulling it, but I didn't know how to get loose. The strained hood squeezed my neck, and it hurt. I began to scream for help as panic set in. I don't think I was there that long before my father came running out in his stocking feet to save me. That was the truth I forgot while hanging from the slide: I wasn't alone. The truth was that my father was near and was just as scared as I was when he saw me.

Many people who struggle with fear feel isolated and ashamed. They believe that no one else has ever felt what they feel. They see themselves as weak and believe that God is disappointed in their lack of "faith." They are uncomfortable with their fear and try to hide it behind sounds of ridiculous laughter or loud anger, which seems more acceptable. They may give great speeches concerning their great faith, and yet are filled with anxiety and fear. If challenged, they will deny their fear and find 101 excuses for it. Most people are ashamed of their fear and don't want to share it with others.

Everyone struggles with fear at some point in her life. There is nothing new under the sun! Satan has been using fear to harass and hinder the church since the beginning of time. In Genesis 3:8-10, he brought fear to Adam and Eve as they opened the gate to his influence through disobedience. Suddenly, they feared the God Who created and loved them. They hid from His punishment. Their sin produced a fear of punishment that drove them from God's Presence. The enemy is using the same tactic to keep people from God's Presence today! I know...

My Testimony

It was nighttime, and I was lying in bed trying to go to sleep. I'm not sure how old I was. My younger sister was about to climb the stairs when she fell and hit her head. She started to cry, and my mother screamed for me to come. I remember my heart felt so tight inside, and it was hard to breathe as I ran to see what had happened. I saw blood all over my sister's face and began to panic. I froze. My mother was trying to care for my sister and sent me to the neighbor's house for help. I screamed and pounded on the door of their house until they came. They immediately got dressed and took my mother and sister to the hospital. As they drove out of the yard, I fell to the kitchen floor, weeping. I felt ashamed that I froze when my mother needed me. I was afraid my sister would die because I took too long to get help. I began to shake and sat on the kitchen floor, rocking back and forth, all alone. Eventually my mother returned with my sister, who had a few new stitches on her forehead. Her situation was not life threatening, though it had seemed so to my child's eye. She was fine...but I was not.

Fear stayed with me. As other events occurred over time, that fear increased. Looking back, I believe the fear of my father dying from his illness had been locked inside for years and had been ignited by my sister's fall. Regardless, I now struggled with nightmares and sleepwalking. My thinking and emotions were confused. I began to lie. Toward the end of my teen years, I experienced panic attacks and bouts of depression that were magnified by the alcohol and drugs that I used to try and hide my fear and shame. No matter how many relationships I had, I felt alone inside. Nothing seemed to help.

At the age of eighteen, I finally received Christ as my true Lord and Savior. However, the panic attacks and depression continued. At nineteen, I suddenly found myself married, living in a street ministry center, and working from morning till night. I tried to lose the fear by focusing on the needs of others. I worked and gave myself tirelessly. But at the age of twenty, the panic attacks increased, and I would again collapse, curled up on the floor in overwhelming fear. When the panic hit, I KNEW I was losing my mind. I wanted to stop, willed myself to stop—but the problem grew worse.

Over the years, I confessed my struggle to several pastors and leaders in hopes of receiving help. They looked at my life and reminded me of the fruitfulness of my labors. Usually, they prayed a brief prayer and then encouraged me to take a vacation. The vacation provided rest for my body, but my soul continued in torment. After a while, I stopped telling anyone about the panic attacks.

When I was twenty-four, we moved to Mt. Pleasant, Michigan to pioneer a new church. My problem escalated. We had no money, little food, and now three babies to care for. We had moved to a college town, and I feared that soon everyone would know how stupid I was. I had no friends. I was incredibly lonely. My husband worked odd jobs, did substitute teaching, and was the entire staff of the new church. In the first few months, my youngest had food poisoning three times from eating donated canned goods that were out-of-date. The spiritual warfare intensified, and I was barely holding myself together. My greatest fear was that one day I would "lose it" and not be able to recover. I wrote letters to my husband and children apologizing in case that happened.

During a fall day, when I took my youngest children for a walk, things finally exploded. I pushed my daughter in a stroller and held my three-year-old's hand as we went to a nearby gas station for a treat. I felt stressed all day and thought the walk would do me good. It was a big mistake. As soon as we entered the store, I felt that everyone was looking at me and knew that I was a mess. I felt afraid and couldn't speak. I grabbed my son's hand and ran out the door. I'm sure we made quite a sight as I ran for the safety of home, pushing the stroller and dragging my poor son along. My daughter fell asleep on the way, and I quickly put her in her crib when we got home. I hoped to get my son down for a nap before the panic attack overtook me completely. My heart was pounding, and I couldn't think.

Suddenly, my son dropped a toy on the floor. The sound woke my daughter, and she began to cry. Everything went dark. The next thing I knew, I was standing over my son who was curled up on the floor in a doorway and weeping softly, "Me sorry, Mommy...me sorry, Mommy..." Shock settled in, and I realized I had become someone who had once frightened me the same way long ago. Self-hate flooded me. I was shaking with fear. I collapsed to the floor sobbing and said, "I'm so sorry," to my son over and over again. To add to the pain, my precious, red-haired boy with his wide blue eyes came to stand beside me and began to gently pat my back while saying, "It's okay, Mommy. You a good Mommy. Me a bad boy." I genuinely wanted to die in that moment.

After comforting my son and getting both children down for a nap, I went to pray in the toy room. I told God that either He would set me free from this fear, or I would leave and never return. I refused to subject my children to my fear any longer. That was the day God supernaturally led me to a couple who prayed deliverance over me. By the next day, I was a new woman. I have never been the same. God restored my battered soul. His Word renewed and restored my mind.

The truths found in this chapter were vital to my recovery. It is TRUTH that sets us free!

"And they heard the sound of the Lord God walking in the garden in the cool of the day, and Adam and his wife hid themselves from the presence of the Lord God among the trees of the garden. Then the Lord God called to Adam and said to him, "Where are you?" So he said, "I heard Your voice in the garden, and I was afraid because I was naked; and I hid myself." And He said, "Who told you that you were naked? Have you eaten from the tree of which I commanded you that you should not eat?" (Genesis 3:8-11)

Many people think that God is angered by their fear. However, God was not angered by the fear that hid Adam and Eve from His Presence. He was grieved. His heart ached for them, and He immediately put a plan into place for their atonement and reconciliation.

Acknowledging Our Fears...

Most Christians believe that God wants them to be strong and courageous every minute of every day. They believe that genuine faith is evidenced with a fearless life and steady emotion. If they struggle with fear, they feel ashamed. They believe their faith has failed God. They begin to interpret the bad things that happen to them as the result of their faithlessness or fear. This opens the gate for fear to increase and the enemy never misses an opportunity. The fear escalates into a feeling of powerlessness, which eventually leads to discouragement, depression, or running away. They know they can't blame God for their fear, so they internalize it. No matter where the fear originated from, they bear the shame of it. In an effort to appease God and make things seem "safe" (and perhaps in an effort to appease or impress man) they mask their fear with "good confessions" and "faith talk." Without realizing it, they are hiding from God's Presence as Adam and Eve did long ago.

God understands our fear. He knows where it originated...in a garden long before we were born. He knows the true source of our fear: a serpent who governs the darkness. God is not angered by our fear. It grieves His heart. He feels the pain of it. His heart aches to intervene.

Giving our fears to God is a process. In my own life, the journey required many steps to freedom:

1) Acknowledging my fears to God

2) Being willing to admit my fears to man without shame or apology

3) Owning fear as MY issue and no longer blaming it upon others

When you read of the life of King Saul in I Samuel, chapters 15-20 you quickly learn he was a fraud. He appeared kingly in stature. He seemed to have a raging temper. But Saul's anger was rooted in fear. He feared the loss of his kingdom. He feared the consequences of his disobedience. He feared giving up control. He feared the anointing and favor he saw on David's life, and he feared the love and loyalty his son felt for David. This fear was masked by angry outbursts and acts of violence, but it could only be stilled in the Presence of God. After venting the anger, Saul was just as miserable as he had been before. Saul's problem was not anger; it was fear.

Taking Off the Mask...

For some unknown reason, people are more comfortable with anger than with fear. It is more accepted in society. People applaud the one who "stands up for himself" but disdains the one who weeps in the corner. Fear is equated with faithlessness, weakness, and failure. No wonder so many are quick to mask their fear with anger!

There is no way to acknowledge fear without a certain level of vulnerability. To some degree, a confession of fear is a confession of weakness. We are admitting we are powerless to erase the emotion; that there are things that we perceive stronger and greater than us; that we are not absolutely sure God can, will, or is able to take care of us; that we need help. It is the last statement that is the hardest to admit.

To those wounded in the past, vulnerability to others is a risk. Positioning them to need someone else opens the door to being hurt again. They fear being taken advantage of. They fear the weakness being used against them in the future. They fear the rejection or abandonment of others who will view them as weak. This was the case with King Saul. He was afraid to admit his need for help and unwilling to be vulnerable to Samuel's correction. He perhaps thought the anger would protect him from loss; but in the end, it cost him everything. So it is with us today. Our unwillingness to admit our fear will allow it to steal much peace and goodness from our lives.

Identifying the Root of Fear...

How can we know if our struggle is fear or something else? Fear manifests itself in many different ways. It may surface as a constant sense of dread and an expectation of trouble. It can become a steady stress and anxiety we become used to living with. If left unchecked, fear can escalate to panic attacks—waves of fear that descend out of nowhere and for no apparent reason. Any sudden occurrence can trigger it. Suddenly, we believe we are losing our minds, are in danger of hurting ourselves or someone else, or are going to die. We become controlling of those we love in an effort to silence our fear of losing them. Some may experience physical symptoms such as back spasms, facial twitches, headaches, stomach or heart spasms, nausea, and more. Obsessive behaviors and phobias are another reaction to fear—another way of seeking to control a fear of harm, attack, sickness, or death. This stress can cause a bloating of the abdomen in very young children, sleeplessness, and nightmares. It breaks God's heart when His children suffer this way...

"But the Helper, the Holy Spirit, whom the Father will send in My name, He will teach you all things, and bring to your remembrance all things that I said to you. Peace I leave with you, My peace I give to you, Let not your heart be troubled, neither let it be afraid." (John 14:26-27)

We are not alone with our fears. Jesus abides with us by His Spirit and brings us His peace. As we allow the Holy Spirit to reveal truth to us, we can be set free from fear. We experience the supernatural peace of God.

It is at this point that many will cry, "Where is the peace???" They have been bound by fear their entire lives. They've tried everything to be free. This has been their problem all along. THEY have tried everything to free THEMSELVES. It simply is not possible.

No one can set himself free from fear. They can sedate it with medication, alcohol, drugs, or hide it behind a million other things; but they cannot rid their lives of it. They can know where the fear came from, the way it manifests in their lives, and the consequences of the torment in their bodies, minds, and relationships. However, they cannot make fear go away. Understanding the fear only positions them to release it to God. Only He can give the peace they long for. To experience the peace, they will have to acknowledge their inability to fix themselves. They will have to ask God to give them His supernatural peace.

The Fear of Punishment...

"If we confess our sins, He is faithful and just to forgive us our sins and to cleanse us from all unrighteousness." (I John 1:9)

Some fear is the result of past sin. We will talk about the need to forgive ourselves in Chapter Seven, but we can deal with the consequence of fear today. If we fear punishment from God, we will not be able to receive His peace. This is the perfect moment to confess your sin to God and receive His forgiveness. Soak in His love for you. Breath in His peace. All is well. Once you have repented of (turned from) all sin, Satan can never again use it against you. It has been supernaturally washed away by the blood of Christ.

If there is a past sin that has opened the door to fear in your life, take some time to write about it in the space on this page. Confess it to God and receive His forgiveness and cleansing today. You don't have to wait to find freedom!

Perfect Love...

"There is no fear in love; but perfect love casts out fear, because fear involves torment. But he who fears has not been made perfect in love." (I John 4:18)

A key to silencing fear in our lives is a revelation of the love of God. When we KNOW God loves us in a personal, committed, unconditional, and affectionate way, we fear nothing! We KNOW God will take care of us. Love won't let Him ignore our cry. Love won't allow Him to turn away from our need. As a loving Father, He cannot stand back when the enemy attacks. God is for us. He loves us. He's near.

Do you KNOW God loves you? If you struggle KNOWING God's love for you, ask the Holy Spirit to reveal it to you. God IS love! He speaks, oozes, and releases love for us every minute of every day. Speak to your emotions and command them to come alive to the love of God in Jesus's

Name. Read the book of John and meditate on Christ's love for you. Let His Word renew your mind. Be filled with God's love!

Perhaps you KNOW God's love for you but fail to understand His power. You KNOW God wants to help you, but you perceive the world or powers of darkness as more powerful than He. Again, ask the Holy Spirit to reveal God's power to you. Read the Gospels and meditate on the powerful acts of God evidenced through Jesus. He is the same yesterday, today, and forever!

After my deliverance so many years ago, there was still a process of renewal to experience. I had to replace old fear-based thoughts and behaviors with God's Word. This took time and effort. There were days when I began to lapse into panic-mode only to discover that I didn't have the energy or actual fear to fuel the anxiety! Instead, I would call a friend and ask her to teach me how a "normal" person responds to stressful situations. Better yet, I learned how God responds and began to respond the same.

Here are some scriptures that may be beneficial to you as you renew your mind:

Leviticus 16:3-8	For the fear of war or tribulation
Leviticus 26:9	For the fear of loss of respect
Leviticus 26:11-12	For the fear of losing God's Presence
Numbers 14:8-9	For the fear of losing God's Presence
Deuteronomy 28:10	For the fear of man and/or attack
Numbers 23:19-20	For the fear of man and/or attack
Psalm 37:4-5	For the fear of losing God's blessing
Deuteronomy 2:24-25	For the fear of losing God's blessing
I Samuel 17:45-47	For the fear of demonic spirits
I Samuel 1:27-28	For the fear of loss of children

II Samuel 6:22	For the fear of commitment
I Kings 4:29-30; 34	For the fear of commitment
Psalm 37:24	For the fear of failure
Psalm 37:3	For the fear of trusting
Matthew 10:28	For the fear of loss of parents
Psalm 23:4	For the fear of evil
Proverbs 10:27	For the fear of evil
Hebrews 2:15	For the fear of death
Psalm 25:14	For the fear of being alone

My Testimony

When my daughter was 10 months old, she nearly died. It was a dark, stormy night. I couldn't sleep and had been lying in bed praying for everyone I knew. I had just finished praying protection over my children when I heard her "cough" in her crib. She was a noisy sleeper, often making noises in her sleep, so I wasn't overly concerned. Suddenly, it felt as if someone were grabbing me by my collar and pulling me out of bed! I felt pushed, running into the nursery as if led by someone else. My mind was reeling, and I thought, "I am really over-reacting!" But when I touched my baby's body, she was clammy and cold.

Flicking on the light, I discovered that my daughter was discolored and gray. There was no breath, no heartbeat, no sign of life. I screamed for my husband and pulled my daughter from her crib. I did everything they teach you to do to revive your child. Nothing worked. Finally, in desperation, I held her by her little arms and shook her with all my might while saying, "In the Name of Jesus, BREATHE!" She gasped, and so I shook her and commanded with the name of Jesus once again. Finally, she began to breathe with her eyes wide open. However, when I touched her eyes, she didn't blink. She was unresponsive. A night and morning in the Emergency Room later and we received the results from the doctor. If I had not "woken up" and checked my daughter, she would have been a case of "crib death."

That night, I rocked her to sleep in her room, too afraid to lay her in the crib. She was so precious, so dear to me! I cried, singing to her and holding her close. Suddenly I saw movement in the doorway. I looked up to see a large angel smiling at me. He nodded his head and waved his hand at me. "Who do you think got you out of bed last night? He gives His angels watch over you." He smiled again and walked down the hall. I realized that God WAS in control and WAS able to care for my family. I put my daughter in her crib and went to sleep in my bed. Knowing God was in control gave me perfect peace.

We can choose to trust. God IS in control. He cares about you. "He [has given] angels charge over you to keep you in all your ways" (Psalm 91:11). You are NEVER alone.

There is a host of angels ready to fight for you. You are
LOVED!

CHAPTER SEVEN

Choosing to Forgive

"I'll hate him till the day I die!"

The young woman was visibly shaking. She was speaking of her father who had sexually abused her throughout her childhood. Eventually he was discovered and spent several years in prison for his crime against her. He had abused other little girls as well. He would never be able to hurt her or anyone else again—he had died in prison from heart disease. He was gone forever… but the wound inflicted on this woman continued to seep with pain and bitterness.

She had been a young teenager when her father's abuse had been discovered. She was certain that seeing him sent to prison would make her "feel better" at last. It didn't. She continued to be tormented with dreams and flashbacks. The bitterness grew and ate away her peace, day and night. When she was a young woman, she determined that if only she could see him face-to-face and tell him how much she hated him—how he had hurt her—she would finally be able to let go and move on with her life. The woman took a trip to the prison and met with her father through bulletproof glass. She vented all of her hatred and bitterness...but he showed no remorse. He didn't seem to care! His face was set in stone. He even smiled! She fled the prison with even greater bitterness inside.

What troubled her most was that her father didn't seem to suffer for the pain he had caused her. The trial hadn't shaken him. The time in prison seemed to be acceptable to him. Her bitter words hadn't moved him at all. Then he died, and there seemed to be no hope of "making him pay" for what he had done. She wanted him to hurt. So she decided to hate him until the day she died. She would never forgive him. She would tell everyone what he had done. She would slander his name at every opportunity. She would make bad choices and make him carry the blame. The woman decided that hating her father was the only way she could find relief from the bitterness that burned inside. But the only one she hurt was herself.

Many people struggle with forgiveness for the same reason this woman did. They feel that forgiveness releases the offender from all responsibility for their actions. They believe that their bitterness or anger is the only tool they have to "hurt" the offender back. They may not say it, but in their heart, they are still waiting to see God's vengeance on the abuser. Some think that forgiving the offender means that they have to renew a relationship with him or her. For these reasons and more, they hold tight to their bitterness, never realizing that they are only wounding themselves.

The truth is that most offenders or abusers are like the woman's father: they are dead to the pain they caused. They are blinded by sin and cannot see the impact of their behavior or words. Their hearts are numbed by their own untended wounds, and they can no longer feel the pain of others. Their "needs" cry louder than the voice of those around them. Even if they seem to show heart-felt remorse after using or abusing others, they will return to it without hesitation. They are imprisoned in their minds and cannot think beyond the limitations of their boundaries. Whether the abuse is verbal, behavioral, physical, mental, or sexual, it flows from the bondage within them. They often separate themselves from the things they do or say. It is not who they "think" they are. Therefore, when confronted with accusations, they sincerely deny any wrongdoing. If they admit to it, they present endless excuses to make the wrong seem right.

You cannot reason with someone who is in bondage. You cannot make them understand. It is as if they speak another language. That is why it is usually fruitless for you to tell them how you feel...how they have hurt you...what they have done. They cannot see it and therefore do not believe it is so. It is not who they think they are. This presents a serious problem if you think you must confront them so that you can "feel better." If they don't respond as you expected; if they show no remorse; if they deny that they hurt you, your wounds are simply intensified. The confrontation costs them very little, but you pay a huge price.

You may be one of the rare ones who confronted an offender and received a good response. You felt a rush of relief afterwards. You believed you were free to move on. Yet your soul is still agitated when you think of the person. You continue to struggle with memories, dreams, or relationship issues that stem from the offense. In the end, your confrontation may have helped the offender to deal with the harm they caused, paying for it with some measure of remorse, but you still feel the pain.

If you are ever going to be free of the past, you will need to forgive those who hurt you. Unforgiveness is like an invisible chain that yokes you to the offender. That is why you may still feel the bitterness and anger long after the offender has been removed from your life or is dead. You may think and speak of the offence as if it happened yesterday. The memories live with every breath you breathe. Forgiveness is not something you do for the abuser; it is something you must do for YOU. There is help to forgive...

"But that you may know that the Son of Man has power on earth to forgive sins—then He said ot the paralytic, 'Arise, take up your bed, and go to your house.' And he arose and departed to his house." (Matthew 9:6)

Jesus answered and said to him, 'If anyone loves Me, he will keep My word, and My Father will love him, and We will come to him and make Our home with him...I in them, and You in Me; that they may be made perfect in one, and that the world may know that You have sent Me, and have loved them as You have loved Me." (John 14:23; 17:23)

Jesus has the power to forgive sin—ALL sin. Only He can see the heart of man and understand why people do the things they do. His supply of love and forgiveness is limitless and complete. There is nothing He can't forgive. The last words He spoke to the Roman soldiers, who had beaten Him beyond recognition and were now nailing Him to a cross, were words of forgiveness (Luke 23:24). When confronted with any offence or abusive situation, He has the power to forgive. It is beyond natural ability...it is supernatural ability. It is His unimaginable power to forgive that gives us hope!

Forgiving the Unforgiveable

God knew that there would be some offences that were humanly impossible to forgive. How could this woman ever forgive a father who used and shamed her for so many years? How could she forgive the mother who allowed it to continue? How could I forgive the young man who molested me or the man who raped me? Some wounds go too deep and are too horrible for us to forgive. This is why God made forgiveness a spiritual act, a supernatural flow of His Divine grace. Forgiveness is not human; it is Divine.

When faced with a wound so deep, a memory so horrible, or abuse so terrible that it is impossible for us to forgive, we can draw from Christ's well of forgiveness. When we are powerless to forgive, He provides His Own forgiveness. From His Presence within, He is able to release a flow of forgiveness that reaches past the unanswered questions and unrepentant abuser and sets our hearts free. All we have to do is ask and we WILL receive (Matthew 7:7). This is His promise to us. It is His goodness that enables us to do what could never do ourselves. Take a moment to drink from His "well" right now...

"Then Peter came to him and said, 'Lord, how often shall my brother sin against me, and I forgive him? Up to seven times?' Jesus said to him, 'I do not say to you, up to seven times, but up to seventy times seven.' (Matthew 18:21-22)

"Therefore, as the elect of God holy and beloved, put on tender mercies, kindness, humility, meekness, longsuffering; bearing with one another, if anyone has a complaint against another; even as Christ forgave you, so you also must do." (Colossians 3:12-13)

"And be kind to one another, tenderhearted, forgiving one another, even as God in Christ forgave you." (Ephesians 4:32)

As Christians, we are told to forgive the offender regardless of the offence. It helps to remember that Christ forgave all of us of our offences, but it does not necessarily enable us to forgive others. We may feel we deserve forgiveness more than the one who offended us. Yet, still we are faced with this command to forgive! The Apostle Peter was certain that Christ must have SOME limitations regarding who and how many times we needed to forgive. Jesus replied with Divine direction: forgive as many times as you are offended.

Forgiveness is not a one-time event. Each offence carried in our memory will have to be addressed over time. There is a bitterness attached to every wound that will need to be cleansed. Keeping a record of past wrongs and harboring a "grudge" against those who wounded us will only result in bondage of bitterness. It helps no one. Accept the need to forgive those who hurt you...not because they deserve it, but because YOU do. Invite the Holy Spirit to invade the memories with His love and forgiveness. Surrender your bitterness to Him. Let it go. Ask Jesus to heal the memories and to give you His forgiveness for the offender. Pray until peace comes...it WILL!

What does true forgiveness look like? It looks like the mind that is set free from the pain of the memories. The memories are yours for a lifetime, but they no longer have power to wound or torment you. It looks like a heart that is free to give and receive love from God and others. It looks like confidence, trust, peace, and a sense of wholeness. You can tell when forgiveness has come, because none of the past or offence will be reflected in the face of the present. Forgiveness sets the person free to pursue life!

Forgiveness does not always end with restored relationship. Relationship with an unrepentant, unchanged abuser/offender will only result in more pain. God does not demand our renewing intimacy with someone who has and will again abuse us. At times, we may continue in a relationship with someone who verbally or emotionally continues to disappoint us; but there will be clear boundaries to ensure that they have no power to abuse us again.

"And forgive us our debts, as we forgive our debtors." (Matthew 6:12)

"Judge not, and you shall not be judged. Condemn not, and you shall not be condemned. Forgive, and you will be forgiven." (Luke 6:37)

Jesus said that we would be forgiven in the same way we forgive others. This can seem an impossible and unfair command to many. Our refusal to forgive others can become an obstacle to our receiving forgiveness from God and others. We live in a world of bitterness. The truth is, many of those who cannot forgive others also find it very difficult to experience forgiveness themselves. Bitterness is the anchor that prevents forward movement in life.

An Honest Heart....

As healing comes to our hearts, the memory of the abuse may shrink in size. Our anger and bitterness sometimes enlarges the scene to justify our depth of emotion towards an offender. Though they did wrong, we may discover that we have judged them for more wrong than they did. Seeing the incidents in truth, without the surge of emotion that surrounded it, helps us to forgive and let go. The difficult thing is admitting that we may have remembered the incident as more than it was. Yet only in admitting and accepting truth can we be set free.

This is especially true when the offence came through disagreement with or disappointment in a close friend or family member. Perhaps there was a verbal fight with unrestrained emotion. There are usually two wounded people in these situations. There are two individuals who offended one another. In the heat of the moment, both behaved badly and/or spoke harshly. There are hurts on both sides. Healing can only come as we own "our" side of the offence and seek forgiveness for ourselves. This may allow the other person to seek our forgiveness as well. Whether they receive our apology or not, we are free from responsibility and able to go on. We can forgive them because we understand our need to be forgiven in the situation.

Ask the Holy Spirit to reveal TRUTH to you concerning the offences of the past. Be open to seeing some things differently than before. Allow Him to adjust your perspective if needed. Sometimes the memories will not change, for they are already established in truth. In other cases, they may "shrink" or change somewhat as truth settles in. Write what the Holy Spirit shows you in the space below and let Him walk you through forgiveness.

It is Okay to Need Help...

The "sinful woman" of Luke 7:36-50 understood her need of forgiveness. She KNEW she was a sinner in need of a Savior. Jesus sat in a room filled with men who needed His love and forgiveness, but only this woman was able to receive. She received because she was willing to acknowledge her sin and seek the help she needed. When forgiveness is sought, it is found at the feet of Jesus! This event marked a brand new beginning for the woman, who became one of the first followers of Jesus. She was able to go and sin no more.

Ultimately, we need to be forgiven. To experience the wonderful freedom of forgiveness, we must first accept our need of it! We must be willing to acknowledge that we have made mistakes. Just as the offender or abuser sinned against us, we have sinned. Perhaps we have made a series of wrong choices, blaming our behavior or speech on the abuse of the past; but this is our choice, not the abusers. No matter who did what to us, we choose what we will do today. We make our own choices. Owning our sin enables us to seek the forgiveness we so desperately need. Seeking forgiveness at the feet of Jesus brings freedom and a brand new beginning.

Are there things you need to receive forgiveness for? Ask the Holy Spirit to reveal truth to you, and record the issues needing Christ's forgiveness in the space below. Then seek the forgiveness you need at the feet of Jesus. You WILL find it!

My Testimony

In an earlier chapter, I shared a testimony of the day I brought my toddler son to tears. He was cowering against a hallway door, saying, "Me sorry, Mommy," over and over again. When I suddenly heard myself screaming at him in the midst of my panic attack, I fell to my knees and began to sob. My rush of emotion and loud voice had frightened my sweet little boy. I was so ashamed. I hated myself. Long after the day was done, and even after I had received deliverance from the panic attacks, I carried the shame of that day. I never stopped hating myself for the pain I caused my precious boy. Although he forgave me completely, and never mentioned it again, I continued to seek his forgiveness and tried to make up for the experience at every opportunity. Eventually, God brought healing to this memory as He led me through a time of repentance. When I finally accepted and received His supernatural forgiveness and was enabled to forgive myself, God, in His mercy, restored my son and healed the wounds of that day. He is so faithful!

One of the greatest hindrances to the healing process is an inability to forgive one's self. Often we cannot let go of bitterness towards others because it is our only way of avoiding the bitterness we feel toward ourselves. We can voice our hatred of others, but we cannot cope with the hatred we feel for own self-loathing. Why did we tolerate the abuse for so long? Why didn't we tell someone? Why didn't we fight back? Why didn't we speak up? Why didn't we walk away? Why did we physically respond to the sexual abuse? What is wrong with us? How could we have been so stupid? These questions end in self-loathing that can only be released by God's supernatural grace. The answers must come, but they are not always easy to receive.

Some of the issues we blame ourselves for are not ours to carry. When the people who abuse us blame their actions or words on us, it is a lie. No one can force others to abuse another. I remember the story of a Christian martyr told long ago. A gun was held to his head, and he was told to torture another prisoner or die. He chose death. Not even the threat of death could force him to abuse his fellow man. Those who sexually or physically abuse others often blame their actions on the victim—that it must have been the way the victim dressed, looked, acted, or something they said that made the perpetrator do it. One child was told that the demon in him made the person beat him so. This again is a terrible lie. Yet often the victims will carry the weight of responsibility for the abuse on their shoulders. If this is the case, the victims will need to forgive themselves and experience God's supernatural grace before they can begin to see the truth and forgive the abusers.

Who is to Blame?

I blamed myself for the decisions others made for most of my life. When they lost their temper, it was my fault. When they made inappropriate remarks or touched me in wrong ways, I knew it was my fault. When they were sad or depressed, it was my fault. When they fought and wouldn't reconcile, it was my fault. When they didn't like how I looked or who I was, it was my fault. When they had a need I couldn't help with, it was my fault.

The weight of all the unfair expectations on my little girl shoulders was one source of the panic attacks I experienced for many years. I cannot count how many times I was told, "Take care of your sister; your mom; your dad— you have to be the big girl and help them more...you are upsetting your mom...you're going to give her a nervous breakdown if you don't stop...your sister needs you to be strong...don't cry; it will upset her...try to cheer him/her up."

People meant well, but they were unknowingly creating a

pressure to take care of everyone; to keep everyone happy.

No person can fix what is broken, wounded, or sick in

another. Only God can do that! But my little girl mind didn't

understand that.

One vivid memory from my childhood encompasses

the pressure I felt. My father was cutting a large branch

from a giant tree that stood in front of our house. He

climbed a long ladder with his saw and began to work. He

told me to hold the ladder so it wouldn't slip. I remember

looking up at him and feeling nervous. I was afraid I

wouldn't be able to hold it—it was swaying beneath his

weight—and that he would fall. Then my fear became

reality. He was suddenly falling towards me and shouted my

name. I jumped out of the way and watched as he hit the

ground with a thud. Blood appeared from his nose, and his

eyes didn't open when I called to him. I ran to my mother in a panic, and she took care of my father who was hurt. I don't remember much of what happened after that. All I could see was my father falling and hearing him call my name. I had failed once again. I blamed myself for his pain and carried that feeling into my adulthood. I was in my thirties before I realized that he didn't fall because of me. The relief I felt!

Believing that I was at fault for everyone's happiness or well-being made me a driven, controlling, and interfering lady. I look back on the way I handled some situations over the years and shudder! I meant well. I wanted to help. I wanted to make everything better for the ones I loved. I wanted to protect them from hurt, from the consequences of their choices, from the hard things of life. When they struggled, I always prayed to find out what I was doing wrong. I believed that it was a fault in me that was allowing them to suffer. If only I could "get it right;" then they would all be happy, healed, or restored. At times, I lost sleep, wept for hours, self-evaluated until my head was spinning. Yet only when God intervened would their situations improve. Miraculously, I began to realize that their issues were often independent of me.

After a season of healing and deliverance, I began to accept my powerlessness to change others. I became comfortable with NOT being able to help. My prayer life increased, and my activity began to slow down. Healthy boundaries were established in relationships. I found a joy and peace I had never known. With God's help, I was able to forgive myself for all the things I had blamed myself for over the years and let them go. I was able to forgive those who had placed blame and unfair expectation on my shoulders. I was able to release control of others to God and began to enjoy the ones I loved. There was no need to "fix" them anymore; that was God's responsibility. Best of all for my family, friends, and co-workers, I became a lot more fun to be and work with!

Have you carried "false responsibility" or unfair expectations on your shoulders? Ask the Holy Spirit to show you. If you have, list them here...

Take time to pray and forgive yourself for the things you've blamed yourself for. Acknowledge your inability to "fix" others. Receive your freedom!

Jesus Understands...

"Therefore, in all things, He had to be made like His brethren, that He might be a merciful and faithful High Priest in things pertaining to God, to make propitiation for the sins of the people. For in that, He Himself has suffered, being tempted, He is able to aid those who are tempted." (Hebrews 2:17-20)

"Seeing then that we have a great High Priest who has passed through the heavens, Jesus the Son of God, let us hold fast our confession. For we do not have a High Priest who cannot sympathize with our weaknesses, but was in all points tempted as we are, yet without sin. Let us therefore come boldly to the throne of grace, that we may obtain mercy and find grace to help in time of need." (Hebrews 4:14-16)

Whatever you have experienced in this life, He understands. He became man and endured abuse, rejection, abandonment, betrayal, pain, and suffering so that He could help us when we hurt. This gives us the confidence to bring anything to Him—to confess any sin or bitterness. We can share our secrets with Him. He is surprised by nothing we say, for He knows all. He has compassion. He will weep with us. He will wrap us in the blanket of His love, and He will never tire of listening.

Christ is our Comforter...but He is also our Healer! He didn't endure the pain only to have an ability to relate to those He loves. He endured the suffering to *end it once and for all* for those who believe! Isaiah 53:1-4 tells us that He corrected all that was wrong at the cross. He reversed every curse, He lifted every weakness and pain, He took the stripes that purchased our physical, mental, emotional and spiritual healing. There was Divine purpose in His suffering. When we pray, He immediately intercedes for us to our Father and arranges for the release of our request. He paid the price for our sin in full. It is ours to take. There is nothing that can prevent us from being set free from the bitterness and pain...nothing but ourselves.

Today you must choose to forgive. No one else can choose this for you. God will not force you to forgive. If you choose to forgive, He will immediately release the grace of forgiveness, just as He promised He would. You may not feel it right away; your heart may seem no different at first...but change will come. As you bask in His Presence day after day, His love will overtake you, and your emotions will align with your choice to forgive. Don't allow the enemy to challenge your decision to forgive no matter what you feel. Your decision will open the door to God's supernatural grace. Jesus will empower you to forgive. Once the decision is made, never look back. Run FREE!

CHAPTER EIGHT

Choosing to Walk in the Spirit

"Be filled with the Holy Spirit…"

(Ephesians 5:18)

What is "normal"? It is hard to define. People define normalcy by their own behaviors and perspectives. For some, it is "normal" for couples to cheat on one another. Others consider it normal to put their fists through walls when angry; while still others believe it normal to struggle with bouts of depression. Once something is defined as "normal," it becomes acceptable to us. This is what life looks like. We no longer resist the behavior or perspective. We make allowances for it in others. We lower any preconceived standard to the acceptable "norm" and accuse those of any other standard of being over-religious, judgmental, or controlling.

Jesus set the bar high for believers. His acceptable "norm" was living in the Spirit. He drew a sharp line between what He considered normal Christian behavior and the world's view. He approved a lifestyle of dependency on God and disapproved a lifestyle of self-sufficiency. He rejected all standards that conflicted with His Fathers. No wonder He was unpopular with the "standard-makers" of His day!

As we choose to release old patterns and perspectives of shame, fear, anger, and bitterness, we will need to replace them with new ways of thinking and behaving. This requires the establishment of new standards for our lives. The old has passed away. All things are becoming new! Yet this is where we will need to exercise our power of choice most carefully. Freedom, once found, needs to be lovingly maintained. Wrong choices made with our newfound freedom can still bring negative consequences to our lives, opening the door to old habits of life. In the same way we relied on God's help in choosing to release negative patterns, we will need to rely on Him to establish the new. We never stop needing Him!

I knew a young woman who grew up in a very restrictive environment. Her parents were controlling and kept the girl at home much of her childhood. They rarely allowed her to participate in group activities for fear of her being "contaminated" by the other youth. They forbid any dating, they selected her friends; the girl was allowed no mind of her own. They made every decision for her. Though outwardly submissive, the girl hated her life.

The day came when the girl graduated from high school and left for college. She had her first taste of freedom! There was no one telling her what to do; she could make every decision for herself. She wanted to try everything that had been denied her. She used her freedom to experiment with drugs and alcohol. She became promiscuous. She skipped classes, quit her part-time job, and blew her financial aid on clothes and music. Then came the day she had to tell her parents that she was pregnant, out of money, and being suspended from school. The young woman had used her newfound freedom to make unhealthy choices that ended in pain.

This young woman had been delivered from the standards of normalcy that her parents held. Her parent's standards were wrong for her. They didn't fit her. In fact, they nearly destroyed her. The standards robbed her of her identity. Yet, when finally tasting freedom from those standards, the girl unwisely adopted the standards of the world around her. She never took the time to observe the outcome of such standards before diving in. She never studied her options because, in youth, they were already set for her. So when she became independent, she had nowhere (or everywhere...) to begin. She never evaluated what was right *for her*. She just ran with the standards of the world.

All her life, she felt abnormal, so the world's ways seemed right; they allowed her a place of identity—even if it wasn't her own.

My Testimony

I was the perfect chameleon. I dressed, spoke, and behaved like whomever I was with. I let the other person dictate my standards. I knew that I was a mess inside. I wasn't sure what I believed or who I was anymore. It seemed right to let others who seemed to know who they were and what they believed set the standards for me. When with church kids, I behaved and spoke "most holy." When with worldly friends, I did whatever they did; I drank, smoked, and did everything else that went along with the partying lifestyle. I rarely made a conscious decision for myself. If I rebelled at home, it was usually after being influenced by a friend. There was always someone else to blame if I never made the decision for myself. It became a pattern of life. I so desperately wanted to "fit in" and be "normal."

When I first became a Christian, I found it much easier to accept Christ as Savior than as Lord. I knew I was a mess. I knew I needed His help and that I needed to be saved! Making Jesus "Lord" was another thing altogether. Letting go of the standards of my friends and holding to the standards of God's Word created a crisis for me. If I stopped living the way others expected, I would seem "abnormal." They would be angry. I knew that holding the standard of Christ would cost me my friends. For a while, I tried to continue my old pattern of pleasing whoever I was with...forgetting that God was always with me! The more I compromised, the more miserable I became. After a time of desperate prayer, I finally made the decision to live only for God. Jesus became my "Lord" for the first time.

I did lose all my friends for a season. It was lonely and a bit depressing. Who wants to hang out with their

MOTHER on a Friday night at the age of 18? I started to study the Bible and went to church regularly. One night I was filled with the Holy Spirit and experienced a surge of God's power that enabled me to stop compromising. I found new joy and peace. *I began to discover my identity.* Slowly, I began to learn how to let the Holy Spirit lead me in my decision-making. God's Word set the standards, and His Spirit led me in a way that allowed me to live those standards in my everyday life. I made many mistakes, but I enjoyed the help of God in overcoming them. I have been, and am still today, a work in progress!

I've been serving God for over 30 years now and am continuing to lean upon the Holy Spirit for help. The end result has been a wonderful life filled with a godly husband, amazing children, beautiful grandchildren, precious friendships, and a cherished church family. I have enjoyed pioneering and directing ministries that have taken me all over the world. I have lived my dreams. The Spirit of God led me on a delightful journey! I can tell you without any hesitation that the benefits of allowing Christ's standards to become my own have far outweighed the price.

"The Spirit of truth, whom the world cannot receive, because it neither sees Him nor knows Him; but you know Him, for He dwells with you and will be in you." (John 14:17)

Jesus told His disciples that the Spirit was WITH them, but would soon be IN them. Jesus was filled with the Spirit of God (John 1:32-34). When He was near, the Spirit was near. The disciples had been walking, talking, eating, and studying Jesus for almost three years. They still didn't understand that the Voice they heard and the power demonstrated through the life of Christ was the Spirit of God. He moved in the power of the Spirit. Now Jesus was promising that this same Voice and power would be in THEM. They would move in the power of the Spirit, too!

Filled with the Spirit!

There are many frustrated people who have prayed a prayer to receive Christ as Savior, severed all ungodly ties, attended church faithfully, and worked hard to adopt Christian standards; YET, they are still making bad decisions resulting in negative consequences. Why? Perhaps this verse provides an answer: They have been near or with the Spirit, but never *filled* with Him. They have stayed near the Presence of God, but have never allowed Him to enter and take over. They are still managing their lives. They are making decisions based on what seems "normal" to them. They are trying to live God's standards without His power. This sets them up for disappointment, for only God can empower us to live His high standards. Perhaps they came to Christ as Savior out of desperation but have never learned how to let Him be Lord. There is a vast difference between Savior and Lord. The first rescues while the second rules.

"But you shall receive power when the Holy Spirit has come upon you, and you shall be witnesses to Me in Jerusalem, and in all Judea and Samaria, and to the end of the earth." (Acts 1:8)

Jesus promised that the disciples would receive power when the Holy Spirit came upon them. This was the same power that worked through the life and ministry of Christ. Only when they received this power would they be able to be His witness—a testimony of Him—in the earth. They could never live His standard of normalcy in their own strength or ability.

"And it shall come to pass afterward that I will pour out My Spirit on all flesh; Your sons and your daughters shall prophesy, Your old men shall dream dreams, Your young men shall see visions. And also on My menservants and on My maidservants I will pour out My Spirit in those days." (Joel 2:28-29)

Suddenly, it happened! Acts, Chapter 2 tells us the story. One morning, as 120 of the believers were gathered in prayer, the Holy Spirit came. He came with the sound of a mighty, rushing wind. He showed Himself in flames of fire that appeared over each head. He took over their speech. He changed the way they lived and spoke. Suddenly, they were empowered to do what they could not do before—to be what they could not be before. The Voice and power of the Holy Spirit was demonstrated through their lives.

People could tell something had changed. These men were living by another standard. Their speech and behavior was "abnormal" to the world's standards. But there was something in this new way—this new standard—that drew the crowd's attention; they were hungry for the experience. They were ready for a new standard of "normalcy" that would give the exuberance and life that was evidenced in the 120. Three thousand received Christ as Savior that very day!

Choosing to Live God's Way...

Most people want freedom from harmful patterns of thinking or behavior. They will wholeheartedly apply themselves to learning how to release the things that hurt them. They are willing to take responsibility for their decisions to let go of their pasts using God's way. However, they are not so eager to make future decisions God's way. They want a freedom that allows them to live their lives their way. This is why so many people who are "saved" during a crisis fail to serve Christ once the crisis is resolved. As soon as the trouble is past, they begin making decisions according to what they want "normal" to be. This usually leads to new crisis situations with negative consequences.

If you are going to continue your healing journey and retain the freedom you've found, you will need to take responsibility for your decisions. You can choose to make decisions dependent on or independent of God. You can choose to lean on the Holy Spirit for help and direction, or you can live your life your way. Only be aware that you will reap the consequences of the choices you make. God will allow you to largely determine your future by the decisions you make.

Choosing to Live in the Spirit...

There are many people who are uncomfortable with the concept of being "filled with the Holy Spirit." They want the Holy Spirit to enter their hearts in a quiet, gentle way that doesn't interfere with their lives or relationships. They want Him to be another addition to their Christian life—but do not want Him invading other areas. Yet there is actually no way for the Spirit of God to enter someone's life without being seen and heard. His Presence is always visible.

When Jesus was filled with the Spirit, John could see Him with his eyes. The heavens opened. The Voice of God was heard. The life of Jesus dramatically changed after that day. Never again did He return to His carpenter's bench. Later, when the 120 were filled with the Holy Spirit, there was a wind that shook the house, a visible manifestation of His Presence in tongues of fire never seen before, and a new language released in their mouths. They spoke in other tongues. The coming of the Holy Spirit upended their lives as He had the life of Jesus three years before. They birthed the first church that day, and their lives were spent in continuing the ministry of Christ.

As you read the Book of Acts, you see other examples of the Holy Spirit at work: healings, signs and wonders, shining lights, shaken rooms, more people speaking in other tongues. The Spirit was visible, evidenced in ways that could be seen and heard. The Holy Spirit was demonstrating His power through the new believers as He had the life of Christ.

If we want the help of the Holy Spirit—if we want Him to enter our lives and demonstrate the love and power of God; if we want His inner guidance and direction as we make our decisions—we will have to prepare ourselves to be turned upside down! He may enter our lives quietly, but He will soon show Himself. He comes to empower us to be witnesses—to manifest the life of Christ. We can speak with "new tongues;" but whether we speak with a new language or not, our speech will be changed. If we submit to His guidance, His Voice will be heard in our mouths and His life evidenced in our standard of living. We won't be able to live "our way" or the old standards anymore. Our lives will be upended! He will give us new purpose, new relationships, and new ways of changing the world we live in.

If you have not yet been filled with the Holy Spirit, you can invite Him to enter in today. Acts 2:38-39 promises that this experience is for everyone who calls upon the Name of the Lord. It is our choice to allow the Holy Spirit to empower us. It requires our decision to receive the leading and guiding of His Spirit in our daily lives. He will never force His will upon us. He allows us the freedom to choose!

"If you then, being evil, know how to give good gifts to your children, how much more will your heavenly Father give the Holy Spirit to those who ask Him?" (Luke 11:13)

"That the blessing of Abraham might come upon the Gentiles in Christ Jesus, that we might receive the promise of the Spirit through faith." (Galatians 3:14)

"And do not be drunk with wine, in which is dissipation; but be filled with the Spirit." (Ephesians 5:18)

The Bible commands us to "be filled with the Holy Spirit." This makes it optional—an experience we can choose to have or NOT to have. He promised to give the Holy Spirit to anyone who asked. Once a person chooses to be filled with the Spirit, they need only ask. When they ask, they

WILL receive (Matthew 7:7). The Spirit (Breath; Wind) of God will enter their lives and change everything!

An Open Door…

When a strong wind blows through an open door, it changes the room it enters! The wind may blow over furniture that has stood in a certain place for generations. It may tear curtains off the windows and knock pictures from the walls. It rearranges everything in the room. However, if the door is shut, the wind is kept outside. The room can then stay as it has always been.

When we receive Christ as Savior, He cleans the "room" of our minds and hearts. He sets everything in order. He revives our dead spirit. He comes to dwell in us. He is with us wherever we go. He hears us. He speaks to us. He has come to make a difference.

When we first feel the Wind of His Presence, we welcome it with open arms. We breathe deep of His life. We love the feeling of His wind on our faces. But when that same wonderful Wind begins to rearrange our thinking or relationships, and begins to sweep away former standards, we often close the door. We want Him to be our Savior, but are unwilling to let Him be Lord. This positions us for a purposeless, powerless existence. Things may stay the same year after year. We never know more freedom, joy, or peace than we knew at the start. Oh, what we miss!

To be filled with the Spirit is to swing wide the door of our hearts and welcome Him in! It is to be revived by the fresh Wind that blows across our lives and to embrace the changes He brings. It is to allow ourselves to be moved by His Wind—His Spirit—wherever He wants to take us. He leads our steps. We still exercise our power of choice every minute of every day as we choose to keep the door open and to submit to His leading; but we are choosing to lean upon Him. Therefore, it is His power that keeps us from falling. It is His force that brings change. All self-effort is abandoned. Normalcy becomes a living dependency upon God every day.

Is your "door" open or close? Are you ready for change? Note your response below.

Romans 8:1-17 promises that when we walk or are led by the Spirit, we have life and peace. He leads us to make decisions that prosper and bless our lives and those around us. He protects us from decisions that will bring only trouble and condemnation to our lives. When we let Him lead, there is no more guilt or shame. This is a good gauge for knowing if we are letting Him lead our decisions. Is there peace and blessing following the choice or trouble and condemnation?

"I say then: Walk in the Spirit and you shall not fulfill the lust of the flesh." (Galatians 5:16)

"But the fruit of the Spirit is love, joy, peace, longsuffering, kindness, goodness, faithfulness, gentleness, self-control. Against such there is no law. And those who are Christ's have crucified the flesh with its passions and desires. If we live in the Spirit, let us also walk in the Spirit." (Galatians 5:22-25)

One of the definitions for walking in the Spirit is to be "occupied" with the Spirit. That means that our minds (our thoughts) are occupied with Him. What is He saying? What is He doing? When we know the answer to these questions, we know easily what decisions need to be made in any circumstance. Again, allowing Him to lead our decisions protects us from doing or saying things that are wrong. He helps us to live *His normal standard* of living. His "norm" becomes our own.

My Testimony

My work often takes me to other countries. At one point, I found myself in Nigeria, stranded at the border of the Republic of Benin. I was to conduct a Children's Ministry Training Seminar in a village about an hour inside the border. It was the first of its kind, and there had been many preparations made. My car was loaded with supplies and gifts to distribute to the pastors, parents, and teachers assembled there. My team was fired up and ready to work. However, after eight hours at the border station, it seemed we were going nowhere!

The officer said we could not cross the border without a specific stamp from the Nigerian office in Lagos. The pastors who had arranged the meeting said that the people would riot and perhaps stone them if I did not come that night. The people had already been waiting all day. The drive to Lagos would take hours, and my Director declared it would take days or even weeks before we could get the specified stamp. I felt tremendous pressure. My heart ached for the people. I didn't know what to do!

The hour was growing late, and my host pastors were becoming more upset. They pleaded with me to go with them. They would show me an illegal way to cross the border. God would want this, they assured me. He would want the people to be ministered to. He would be pleased by my willingness to risk being arrested to serve the people. They wept and begged. By now, my head was spinning.

Suddenly, the officer changed his tone of voice. He smiled and behaved as a friend, offering to turn his back so I could cross the border illegally. He assured me it would be fine. This made the host pastors more insistent, and they increased their pressure for me to come.

So many voices! I finally turned my back to everyone and laid my face on the hood of the car with my arms outstretched in prayer. I began to cry out for the wisdom of God. At that moment, Holy Spirit reminded me of a prophetic word that had been given at my church prior to the trip. The Spirit had prophesied that there would be a time on the trip when I wouldn't know what to do and I was not to listen to the voice of man. I was to do as **He** led. In the next moment, I knew what the Spirit was leading me to do. The host pastors began to wail as I announced that I was returning to Lagos for the stamp. I would send my Director's wife to begin the promised training that night while we drove. The Lord would provide the stamp in the morning, and we would be at the meeting that day. The pastors hustled the Director's wife and supplies into their cars with grim looks on their faces, and I could see that not even my Director believed I would get the stamp. It was a quiet ride back to Lagos.

The next morning we received the specified stamp on my passport and drove back to the border. The officer was furious to see that we were now able to pass the border legally. His plan to "turn his back" long enough to catch me illegally crossing the border backfired. No arrests would be made! We drove to the meeting and were greeted with shouts of praise! The Holy Spirit had orchestrated a miracle! All I had to do was let Him lead.

"But when the Helper comes, whom I will send to you from the Father, the Spirit of truth who proceeds from the Father, he will testify of Me." (John 15:26)

"However, when he the Spirit of truth, has come, He will guide you into all truth; for he will not speak on His own authority, but whatever He hears he will speak; and He will tell you things to come." (John 16:13)

"But as it is written: Eye has not seen, nor ear heard, nor have entered into the heart of man the things which God has prepared for those who love Him. But God has revealed them to us through His Spirit. For the Spirit searches all things, yes the deep things of God. For what man knows the things of a man except the spirit of the man which is in him? Even so, no one knows the things of God except the Spirit of God. Now we have received, no the spirit of the world, but the Spirit who is from God, that we might know the things that have been freely given to us by God." (I Corinthians 2:9-12)

The Holy Spirit is our Helper and guides us into all truth. He knows what's coming and can prepare us. He knows the best way to glorify Jesus in every situation. He reveals God's plans and purposes. We need Him!

No Longer Survivors...

For those who have been wounded or abused, it is often difficult to admit "needing" anyone. Needing someone makes us vulnerable to being used or disappointed. Abuse victims often call themselves "survivors," meaning that they take care of themselves. They rely on no one. They make things happen for themselves. They don't let anyone control them. They thrive on their independence.

Survivors are determined to protect themselves from more pain. If they build walls around themselves and never depend on anyone else, they believe they will be protected from being hurt again. But the very walls they build to protect themselves serve as prisons. They are isolated, lonely, and without help. And one person alone can never fend off trouble coming from four different directions! We were created to need others.

No matter who we are, we don't know everything. We don't have all wisdom and counsel. We have not experienced all there is in life. We don't have a full understanding of the spirit realm. We need the Helper to help us! He knows all, has experienced all, and has full understanding. There is no one better to give direction to our lives than He. The Holy Spirit gives the best counsel. We need only ask, listen, and let Him lead.

Being Honest with God...

If you struggle trusting God, tell Him so. Ask Him to help you. Let Him heal the wound that challenged your trust. Allow Him to wash away the fear of trusting again. II Corinthians 3:17-18 promises that we can be transformed by the Spirit of God. He can change our expectation. He can alter our perspective. He brings a freedom to love and trust; a freedom to receive the help we need. Take a moment to talk to Him right now...

FINAL THOUGHTS

Some might wonder why I chose this book to be published first when my file drawers are filled with other manuscripts. Re-reading it during the editing process often made me wonder the same thing! Why tell the world about a past long forgiven and forgotten? Why revisit the painful mistakes and experiences that Jesus healed and covered so many years ago? I'm not the woman I once was. I've been redeemed! That's WHY I chose to publish this book. The words on these pages flowed out of my healing journey, often copied directly from my personal journal as I prayed and processed my struggles in my favorite chair at home. My life wasn't perfect. There was pain. I made many mistakes. BUT my story didn't end there!

My life before Christ was only the beginning of my story. My fear, shame, and anger were chapters in my book of life. When I met Jesus, a whole new chapter began, and every page turned has revealed greater freedom, joy, and peace. I know who and Whose I am. In Him, I have found identity, purpose, and a Love worth living for. I can't wait to see how the story ends!

I want YOU to know that your story isn't over. You have many chapters to live. And the choices you make will determine what is written on the pages. It doesn't matter how sad, bad, or dark your beginning was. If you will put the pen in God's hand, he will turn your life into a beautiful testimony that will impact all who know you.

There will be no sequels to *The Power of Choice*. There are no more secrets I need to tell. I was lost—oh SO lost! But now I am found! I WAS blind, but now I see! I refuse to keep looking over my shoulder at a past that I've been set free from. I refuse to allow that same past to dictate my future. I am a new creation. I am a child of the King. I am living the life He always intended for me.

Live the life He intended for you. Take back your right to choose. Choose love. Choose joy. Choose forgiveness.

Choose your way to freedom! I believe with all my heart your story will have a happy ending.

Let a new chapter begin today!

If you would like to share your story with me, write to:

HCI Founder, Carla Ives

Heart Cry International

PO Box 207

Mt. Pleasant, MI 48804 USA

Or contact me through our website at:
www.heartcryinternational.com

Run Free!

ABOUT THE AUTHOR

Carla Ives is the Founder and CEO of Heart Cry International, a non-profit organization offering Christian discipleship training & materials with humanitarian aid to impoverished children around the world.

www.heartcryinternational.com
PO Box 207, Mt. Pleasant, MI 48804
989-506-8993
cives@heartcryinternational.com

Made in the USA
Middletown, DE
07 November 2023

42099908R00128